HOW TO WRITE A WINNING PERSONAL STATEMENT FOR GRADUATE AND PROFESSIONAL SCHOOL

HOW TO WRITE
A WINNING
PERSONAL
STATEMENT FOR
GRADUATE AND
PROFESSIONAL
SCHOOL

THIRD EDITION

RICHARD J. STELZER

Peterson's
Princeton, New Jersey

Visit Peterson's Education Center on the Internet (World Wide Web) at
http://www.petersons.com

Library of Congress Cataloging-in-Publication Data

Stelzer, Richard J.
    How to write a winning personal statement for graduate and professional school
  / Richard J. Stelzer.
      p.   cm.
    ISBN 1-56079-855-6
    1. College applications—United States.   2. Universities and colleges—Graduate
work—Admissions.   3. Professional education—United States—Admission. I. Title.
LB2351.52.U6S74 1997
378'.1056—dc19   88-37443
                                                                            CIP

Editorial direction by Erika Pendleton   Composition by Gary Rozmierski
Copyediting by Jennifer Stern   Creative direction by Linda Huber
Proofreading by Joanne Schauffele   Interior design by Cynthia Boone

Printed in Canada

10 9 8 7 6

CONTENTS

PREFACE

O f all the tasks you face when applying to graduate or professional school—from choosing universities to preparing for and taking standardized tests, from soliciting recommendations to having transcripts sent out—writing the personal statement(s) is among the most formidable. With the keen competition for admission to graduate schools, the personal statement or autobiographical essay often becomes a crucial element of the application package. This book provides a wide array of information and suggestions that should make preparation of your personal statement easier, less intimidating, and more successful.

At the back of this book you will find a set of exclusive, revealing interviews with a group of admissions professionals from more than two dozen of the nation's top-tiered law, business, and medical schools, as well as other selected graduate programs. With candor and clarity, these professionals disclose what they look for in personal statements, describe the mistakes applicants commonly make, and offer advice on how to make your statements as effective as possible. In conjunction with the information, exercises, and advice provided on the following pages, their comments should prove an invaluable resource to you.

Naturally, nothing in this book shall be construed as guaranteeing any applicant admission to any graduate or professional school.

PART 1:

INTRODUCING . . . YOU

A personal statement or autobiographical essay represents a graduate or professional school's first nonnumerical introduction or exposure to you, to the way you think, and to the way you express yourself. There might be interviews later on (for medical school applicants and some others), but for now, in the beginning of the application process, the personal statement alone must serve as a reflection of your personality and intellect. You must sell yourself through this statement, just as you would attempt to do in a job interview, and preparation and thought are essential.

As hard as it is to write in general, it is even more difficult to write about oneself. So don't be discouraged; as a consultant who has advised many applicants, I can assure you that everyone has problems composing these statements. If you have a friend who cranks one out in two hours flat with no agonizing over what he or she is writing, chances are it's not a statement that will do much to enhance the prospects for admission. Good ones take time. Bad ones can sabotage your chances for success.

The personal statements or essays required of graduate and professional school applicants fall into two major categories. There is the general, comprehensive personal statement, which allows the applicant maximum latitude in terms of what he or she writes. This is the type of statement often prepared for the Personal Comments section of the standard medical school application form. It is also the kind of statement that many law school applicants elect to write.

The second category encompasses essays that are responses to very specific questions, such as those found on business school and other graduate application forms. Here you might have less latitude in terms of the content of your essay(s), but it is still possible and prudent to compose a well-considered and persuasive response that holds the reader's interest.

No matter what type of application form you are dealing with, it is extremely important that you *read each question carefully and make every effort to understand it and respond to it.* Whatever else you choose to discuss in your essay, you must be certain to address the specific question that the application poses. Some applications are more vague or general in their instructions than others; for these it is often possible to compose almost any sort of essay you wish. In these instances it is almost as if you are participating in the dream interview, in which you both ask and answer the questions. You have virtually total control, and you also have a remarkable opportunity that you can either maximize or squander—the choice is yours.

It is crucial to understand that even graduate schools offering the same degree often have very different requirements with respect to the personal statement(s). For example, there *are* some law schools that expect essays to revolve around the issue of why you wish to attend law school (or become a lawyer). Many law schools, however, very deliberately avoid asking that question because they are bored with the generally homogeneous responses it tends to provoke, or simply believe another question (or type of statement) provides them with a far more interesting and revealing look at their applicants. For the latter law schools, the applicant's motivation for studying law becomes almost a peripheral issue.

Understand and Explain Yourself

The most surprising—and damaging—error that many would-be law students, medical school candidates, and other applicants make is failing to take a very thorough, probing, and *analytical* look at themselves and their objectives. Admissions committee members are looking for interesting, insightful, revealing, and nongeneric essays that suggest you have successfully gone through a process of careful reflection and self-examination.

Set Yourself Apart

By "nongeneric" I mean a personal statement that only *you* could have written, one that does not closely resemble what all other applicants are likely writing. You come up with this type of statement by being *personal* and *analytical*. You could achieve the former by including information rarely shared with others and the latter by assessing your life more critically than usual. In any event, a personal and analytical approach is key to success in this endeavor.

AN IMPORTANT EXERCISE

In order to begin writing your personal statement—your story—you'll need the answers to some basic questions. Pretend you have five minutes to speak with someone from an admissions committee. This person asks, "What's most important for us to know about you?" You must make a case for yourself and hold the listener's interest. What would you say? Figuring that out, determining what you would say, is a challenge that is critical to your success in preparing an effective statement. Answering the following questions will facilitate this task, but be patient with yourself—this is a difficult exercise.

Questions to Ask Yourself

- What's special, unique, distinctive, or impressive about you or your life story? What details of your life (personal or family problems/ history, any genuinely notable accomplishments, people or events that have shaped you or influenced your goals) might help the committee better understand you or help set you apart from other applicants?

- When did you originally become interested in this field and what have you since learned about it—and about yourself—that has further stimulated your interest and reinforced your conviction that you are well suited to this field? What insights have you gained?

- *How* have you learned about this field—through classes, readings, seminars, work or other experiences, or conversations with people already in the field?

- If work experiences have consumed significant periods of time during your college years, what have you learned (leadership or managerial skills, for example), and how has the work contributed to your personal growth?

- What are your career goals?

- Are there any gaps or discrepancies in your academic record that you should explain (great grades and mediocre LSAT scores, for example, or a distinct improvement in your GPA if it was only average in the beginning)?

- Have you had to overcome any unusual obstacles or hardships (e.g., economic, familial, physical) in your life?

- What personal characteristics (integrity, compassion, persistence, for example) do you possess that would enhance your prospects for success in the field or profession? Is there a way to demonstrate or document that you have these characteristics?

- What skills (leadership, communicative, analytical, for example) do you possess?

- Why might you be a stronger candidate for graduate school—and more successful and effective in the profession or field—than other applicants?

- What are the most compelling reasons you can give for the admissions committee to be interested in you?

It won't be easy to answer all of these questions, but this is an exercise that will have great practical benefit in readying you to write an outstanding personal statement.

Probably at least part of the answer to the question "What's most important for the admissions committee to know about you?" will be contained in the first paragraph of your essay. But one thing is certain: Once you complete your essay, you will know exactly what you would say in that hypothetical meeting with the admissions committee member. If you've written the essay in the correct way, you will have thought about yourself, your experiences, and your goals and formulated an interesting and persuasive presentation of your story.

TELL A STORY

The personal statement is (in many cases) just that: a sort of story. By that I *don't* mean that you should fabricate or invent *anything*; be truthful and stick to the facts. What you should do, however, is think in terms of telling a story. If your statement is fresh, lively, different—not to mention articulate—you'll be putting yourself way ahead of the pack. Why? Because by distinguishing yourself through your story—by setting yourself apart from other applicants—you'll make yourself *memorable*. If the admissions committee remembers you because what you wrote was *catchy* (without being inappropriate), you have an obvious advantage; much of what is submitted to the committees is distressingly homogeneous and eminently forgettable, if not sleep-inducing.

It never hurts if the story you tell has drama. Some people have life stories that are inherently dramatic. For example, here in the United States there are many applicants who have come from other countries, often settling in a new homeland with no money, connec-

One of the worst things you can do with your personal statement is to bore the admissions committee, yet that is exactly what most applicants do.

tions, or knowledge of the language or culture. Such circumstances, which obviously apply only to a minority of applicants, constitute dramatic obstacles that the applicant has had to overcome to reach his or her present position. But you do not have to be foreign-born to have experienced some sort of challenge or difficulty that could be relevant, absorbing, and—if properly presented—memorably dramatic. (The latitude you have in composing your essay obviously depends on the question asked.)

Find an Angle

If you're like most people, however, your life story might well lack significant drama, so figuring out a way to make it interesting becomes the big challenge. Finding an angle or "hook" is vital. For example, a law school applicant with ordinary grades but outstanding credits in other areas might choose to present herself as follows, emphasizing exceptional athletic prowess and relevant work experience in order to distinguish herself: "As a former college tennis star, now playing on the women's professional circuit, I am in a position that many athletes would covet. If I want, I can earn a living in pro sports. For most, this would be a dream come true. In my own case, however, I have decided—after working as a paralegal in a law firm—that I can make a more significant mark as an attorney, winning my battles not on tennis courts but in courts of law." This would provide an offbeat and memorable introduction to such an applicant's story.

Concentrate on Your Opening Paragraph

Keep in mind when composing your statement that the lead or opening paragraph is generally the most important. It is here that you grab the reader's attention—or lose it. Once you figure out this first paragraph, the remainder of the essay should be less problematic because you will have a framework for what you're going to say. If there's drama to your statement, it will be introduced in the opening paragraph so that the reader is eager to continue. If you're telling some sort of story, you'll use this first paragraph to introduce the elements most relevant to that story—and the ones that will hold greatest interest for the reader.

Tell Who You Are

Beyond the first paragraph or two, there might be an elaboration on material introduced earlier, or simply further distinguishing information relating to your background and experiences. The committee should be getting a sense of who you are, what makes you tick, and how you are different from other applicants. They should be interested in you by now, eager to hear more, impressed that what you're saying to them—the story you're relating—is not simply what they've read a thousand times before.

Later in your personal statement you might want to detail some of your interest in or exposure to your particular field. You might say something to suggest to the committee that you have a realistic perception of what this field or profession entails. Refer to experiences (work, research, etc.), classes, conversations with people in the field, books you've read, seminars you've attended, or any other sources of specific information about the career you want and why you're suited to it.

Sometimes a personal statement can be perfectly well written in terms of language and grammar, but disastrous in lacking punch or impact and in being totally off the mark concerning what it chooses to present about the applicant. Remember, what's most important about your personal statement is *what you say* and *how you say it!* Be *selective* about what you tell the admissions committee. Often you are specifically limited to a certain number of pages (two double-spaced typed pages—or just over—should suffice for most applicants, unless multiple questions require more space), so it is necessary to pick and choose in relating your story. What you choose to say in your statement is, again, very much a reflection of *you* because it shows the committees what your priorities are, what you consider to be important. For this reason, the personal statement is often an indication, too, of your *judgment,* so be careful and give a great deal of thought to what you write. Much thinking—probably over a period of *weeks*—should, ideally, precede the writing. Think about yourself, your background, experiences, and abilities—as well as what you know about the profession—and develop a strategy.

Review Your Personal History

Applicants preparing personal statements very often fail to remember or include facts (experiences, events, achievements) that are extremely relevant, either to their career choice and application or in terms of explaining what makes them tick. One law applicant almost forgot that he had spent a summer working for an assistant district attorney—the most potent, relevant, and interesting weapon in his arsenal! It sounds unbelievable, but this occurs all the time. Another law school applicant almost forgot to tell the admissions committees of his experience as chief defense witness in a criminal trial. My suggestion: *Review your life very carefully* (get help from family or friends if necessary) for facets or experiences that reveal an unusual dimension, relate to your professional goals, or could serve as evidence of your suitability for a certain career (the Preparatory Questionnaire at the back of this book will be very helpful to you).

What Not to Include

There are certain things that normally are best left out of personal statements. In general, references to experiences or accomplishments during your high school years or earlier are not a good idea. There are exceptions, I am sure (if there was an extraordinary achievement or traumatic event that had a significant impact on your development or career plans, go with it), but as a rule, introducing material from this period of your life can make your statement seem sophomoric, at a time when you *should* want to come across as a mature young adult (or as even more sophisticated if years have intervened since your undergraduate work).

Don't mention subjects that are potentially controversial; it is impossible for you to know the biases of members of various admissions committees. Religion and politics normally don't belong in these statements, although, again, there may be exceptions (an applicant who has held an important office on campus or in the community would likely want to include this fact). Personal political views usually are not appropriate for personal statements. Any views that might be interpreted as strange or highly unconventional should also be omitted because you want to avoid the possibility of offending any of the individuals in whose hands the fate of your graduate school application rests.

Sometimes there will be things you want to mention because you are proud of them, perhaps justly so. At the same time, though, there are achievements and experiences that do not belong in your statement, not because you're hiding anything but because you're being *selective* about what you write. Don't pull something out of left field—something that doesn't fit into the story you're telling or the case you're trying to build—just to stroke your own ego. Be smarter than that. Again, *be selective!*

Reviewing What's Been Said (Plus a Few New Points)

Let's review some of the points we have presented up to now, as well as a few additional thoughts (and questions) for you to consider.

- Remember that, in a general sense, what's most important is what you say and how you say it.

- Whatever else you do, be sure to answer the question(s) the admissions committee is asking.

- Determine what you would tell an admissions committee member if you had five minutes to answer the question "What's most important for us to know about you?" This exercise will force you to do the type of thinking that must precede the preparation of an

> **Don't make the mistake of trying to guess what the admissions committee is looking for, and don't just write what you think the committee wants to hear. Such ploys are highly obvious to admissions people and can be detrimental to your cause.**

effective personal statement. For help, refer to the list of questions you should ask yourself.

- When appropriate, find an angle and tell a story about yourself. If your life story has drama, use it.

- You are preparing a *personal* statement. Often it is appropriate and useful to include material that is quite personal in nature.

- Grab the reader's attention in your opening paragraph.

- Review your life carefully—with outside help, if necessary—to make certain you're including all relevant information. (See the Preparatory Questionnaire at the back of the book.)

- Be selective. Don't introduce inappropriate material or get into so much detail that your judgment can be called into question.

- Try to maintain a positive and upbeat tone. While it is often useful to deal candidly with aspects of your history that might be perceived negatively, overall you still want to project confidence and enthusiasm.

- Be specific when appropriate.

- Avoid potentially controversial subjects.

- Express yourself clearly and concisely.

- Adhere to stated word limits.

- Be meticulous (type and proofread your essay carefully).

A lot of the real superstars have failed miserably at times. We think the best candidates are ones who have failed and learned from it.

- If a school wants to know why you're applying to it rather than another school, do a bit of research if necessary to find out what sets your choice apart from other universities or programs. If the school setting would provide an important geographical or cultural change for you, this might be a factor to mention.

- *Think* about what you're saying. (Is it interesting, relevant, different, memorable?)

- Be honest. Are you being yourself and revealing yourself? In many instances, admissions people are interested in finding out about who you are, and they appreciate honesty and candor. (One representative from a leading business school even told me that he likes to hear about applicants' setbacks because "through events like that, we see a lot of the qualities of rebounding. A lot of the real superstars have failed miserably at times. We think the best candidates are ones who have failed and learned from it.")

- Are you providing something more than a recitation of information available elsewhere in the application?

- Are you avoiding obvious clichés? For example, a medical school applicant who writes that he is good at science and wants to help other people is not exactly expressing an original thought. (One law school admissions representative told me, "When we discuss mistakes, we jokingly refer to the person who starts out a personal statement with a quote, either from de Tocqueville or from Shakespeare, such as the one that says, 'The first thing we do, let's kill all the lawyers.'")

- Use the Evaluative Questionnaire yourself (in addition to giving it to others) to assess the effectiveness of your rough draft.

WHAT YOU MUST KNOW ABOUT BUSINESS SCHOOL APPLICATIONS

Business school applications merit special attention because, unlike those for most medical and law schools, they tend to bypass the single, comprehensive personal statement in favor of a series of essays. Business schools typically require responses to a minimum of two to three questions, with some schools asking for considerably more. This is clear evidence of the great importance that business schools attach to this part of the application.

The application which for years has attracted particular attention due to its unusually high number of required essays is that of Harvard Business School. Formerly there was some speculation that this was partly a way of that institution's compensating for not requesting or accepting GMAT scores. However, even now that the GMAT requirement has been reinstated at Harvard, the school has still been opening eyes with a daunting seven mandatory essay questions. This circumstance would seem to underscore the substantial weight still given to the essays at Harvard—as well as other business schools—in determining those applicants who will gain a coveted spot in the entering class.

Confronted with so many different questions for which business schools expect impressive responses that are thoughtfully conceived, well-written, and reasonably sophisticated, MBA applicants find themselves with an enormous amount of work to do. Self-assessment is a big part of this process, as is a careful review of both your life and what you have done professionally. In my consulting practice, I often work with very successful individuals who have never before had to articulate in any substantive way exactly what they do. Now, in applying to business school, these clients for the first time must communicate this information in a very clear, concise, powerful manner that is immediately accessible to anyone, even without knowledge of the applicant's field. Being able to convey both the substance and significance of what one does (or has done) in one's work life is crucial for all applicants.

Keep in mind that the whole process of preparing these essays effectively will be of incalculable benefit to you later on, when your business school interviews take place. Candidates who do a good job with their essays invariably have learned more about how to explain and present themselves, and thus typically bring greater confidence and skill to the interview situation.

A positive trend in business school applications is the increasing availability of an optional essay for discussing important, relevant material which the other essays have not provided an opportunity to introduce. Used with discretion, this optional essay can, for some individuals, be invaluable.

While applying to a variety of MBA programs is always a time-consuming challenge, mitigating this problem sometimes, to a certain degree, is the fact that there often tends to be at least some overlap in questions posed by different business schools. (However, this observation comes with a qualifier and a caveat; see the Special Advice paragraph at the end of this section.) So while the phrasing of the question may vary from school to school, an inquiry about why the applicant has decided to seek an MBA, for example, can appear on application after application. (The prevalence of this particular question, incidentally, would seem to suggest that the business schools are very interested not only in how applicants express themselves and defend the merits of their candidacy for an MBA program, but also in how they explain their educational and professional plans.)

Over the years several business schools have asked questions concerning ethical dilemmas the applicant may have faced, some wanting to know the applicant's choice of action, others not. Michigan and, more recently, the Fuqua School have posed complex situational ethics questions which seem to seek similar insights.

Wharton was in the vanguard of those business schools posing unusual questions, at one point in the 1980s even asking applicants what nine items they would choose to take along on a solo space flight and why. Recently, however, the school's questions have been somewhat more conventional.

Innovative, provocative, and challenging essay questions or requests still continue to appear on many business school applications, and the following represent some recent examples:

- *Submit your own interview report providing us an assessment of the following attributes: maturity, creativity, problem-solving skills, interpersonal skills, leadership potential, sense of purpose, and your recommendation to the Admissions Committee.* (Sloan School/MIT)

- "The unexamined life is not worth living."–Plato. *In light of the above quotation, please discuss a decision you have made which, in retrospect, has had a profound influence on your present circumstances. In hindsight, would you have made a different decision? Please explain.* (Haas School/Berkeley)

- *Write a newspaper article you might read in the year 2020.* (Chicago)

- *It's August in the new century and you have three years of experience with the company that hired you after you earned your MBA. Layoffs, mergers, and acquisitions continue to define the business climate. You've just learned that your position will be eliminated. You don't have the seniority required for severance pay or outplacement services but will receive your salary through September 15. What is your plan of action?* (Stern School/NYU)

- *What do you believe to be the most important trend or pivotal event in your profession over the past five years?* (Fuqua School/Duke)

- *Describe a failure and how you dealt with it.* (Darden School/Virginia)

- *Be your own career counselor. What aspects of your personality or background present the greatest obstacle(s) to achieving your goals?* (Kellogg/Northwestern)

- *Tell us about a risk you have taken (personal or professional). What was your motivation behind taking it, and what was the ultimate outcome? What obstacles, if any, did you face?* (The Anderson School/UCLA)

- *Each of us has been influenced by the people, events, and situations of our lives. How have these influences shaped who you are today? (Our goal is to get a sense of who you are, rather than what you've done.)* (Stanford)

- *Imagine that through the marvels of technology, you have the ability to relive one day of your life. What day would you choose? Why?* and *Ten years after graduating from the Michigan MBA program you are the subject of a magazine article. In what magazine would the article appear and why? What would the article say about your achievements and goals?* (Michigan)

- *How would you characterize the effect of your contributions to the groups or organizations in which you have participated?* (Yale)

More common questions deal with the applicant's most significant accomplishments, professional progression to date, career goals, examples of leadership, and outside interests.

Special Advice: Some business schools' questions at first glance seem similar but are not really the same. Don't fall into the trap of 1) not noticing nuances that make a difference and affect the way the question must be answered; and 2) sending identical essays to different schools despite the fact that their questions are not actually exactly alike. Admissions officers at major business schools usually know what other top MBA programs are asking applicants, and they are unfavorably impressed when a candidate submits another school's essay to them.

PART II:

WINNING PERSONAL STATEMENTS

What you will read on the following pages is a series of successful personal essays—ones that helped their writers gain acceptance to graduate school. Notice the way in which many of the applicants have used an angle and told a story about themselves. In some cases they have used drama in their presentations to catch the reader's interest and set themselves apart from other applicants. When there were obstacles they had to overcome in their lives, these were clearly delineated in the personal statement. There is something in almost all of these essays that distinguishes the applicant and stands out in the reader's mind afterward. The applicants reveal themselves as reflective, analytical, self-knowing, and articulate.

In presenting these examples of successful essays, it is not our intention that you copy from this material in your own application.

AT FIRST GLANCE, THE MOST remarkable thing about me might seem to be the fact that I have the temerity to apply to law school in the first place. I have a blemished academic record that includes both withdrawals and failing grades, and by the time I receive my degree in May, I will have spent six years as an undergraduate. Looking beyond these statistics, however, to the harrowing circumstances of my personal life, it quickly becomes clear that what is much more remarkable is the fact that I have survived at all. In retrospect, I see that I could easily have been crushed by all that happened, that I could have lost all hope, belief in myself, and ambition. Somehow, fortunately, something within me has prevented that from occurring.

With my parents and two younger sisters, I came to America from Asia when I was eight. We were poor from the time we arrived (my father first worked as a janitor, my mother as a seamstress), but I hardly knew the difference as a young child. I was aware that my mother arose each morning at five to take a bus to work, and I knew that I was responsible for taking care of my sisters in her absence. In fact, I was a virtual surrogate parent, assuming a key role in raising my sisters.

Eventually my father bought a small gas station, where from the age of 12 I helped out each day by pumping gas. I would go to work right after school and not come home until midnight. On weekends I worked from nine to nine.

When I was ready to attend college, my parents had somehow saved enough money to underwrite the cost. My freshman year–when, for the first time, I did not have to work–I had a 3.8 GPA. This was more reflective of my academic potential than the grades I earned in subsequent years, when family problems made it impossible for me to concentrate on my studies. My father's business was going steadily downhill (at times he did not even have enough money to buy gas for

At first glance, the most remarkable thing about me might seem to be the fact that I have the temerity to apply to law school in the first place. I have a blemished academic record that includes both withdrawals and failing grades, and by the time I receive my degree in May, I will have spent six years as an undergraduate.

the station), and my family needed my help in order to survive. I began working 35 to 40 hours a week selling men's clothes. Nevertheless, my family's economic picture deteriorated steadily. The five of us moved into a two-bedroom apartment because that was all we could (barely) afford. My father lost his business, and my college notified me that I was "disenrolled" because I was unable to pay my tuition. By the following semester I had saved enough to return to school, but times were still difficult. Occasionally we had no gas or electricity in our apartment because bills were having to go unpaid. At one point we even had to go three days without food. Then, in late April, disaster struck. My family was evicted from its apartment, with the landlord temporarily refusing (illegally) to let us back in to retrieve our possessions. For two weeks I slept in the library at my school, while my parents slept on the floor of a building that was being remodeled. (Both of my sisters were away at college.) The eviction preceded my finals by two weeks and, not surprisingly, had a devastating impact on my performance.

I realize that the poverty in my background is not unique, that other applicants have likely had to deal with similar problems. However, as the only son in an Asian family, I always had a greater-than-usual amount of responsibility on my shoulders. It is difficult for me to convey the humiliation and pain I felt over the years

> **It is difficult for me to convey the humiliation and pain I felt over the years as I watched my parents assume demeaning roles, exacerbated by their poor command of English and ignorance of their rights. Their experience has made a deep impression on me and sensitized me to the problems and injustices which so many suffer.**

as I watched my parents assume demeaning roles, exacerbated by their poor command of English and ignorance of their rights. Their experience has made a deep impression on me and sensitized me to the problems and injustices which so many suffer. It is important to me that I be able to lead a life that is noble and worthwhile, and I want to do this by being in a position in which I can help others and make a contribution. I plan to do this through a career in law.

For nearly three years I have been involved with a nonprofit organization created to help preserve and protect the rights of the Asian-American community. My participation in this group has helped focus my interest in eventually applying my legal skills toward the end of serving those in the Asian-American community. In fact, I became chairman of the group's legal committee, for which I organized two free legal seminars with the Asian-American bar organization. Last year I also helped raise more than $66,000 as fundraising chairman for the group. And currently I am working with yet another legal resources group as a member of the board of directors of an association formed to protect low-income tenants from the dangers of prepayment of loans by building owners.

    I realize that, given my academic record, I am going against the odds in applying to law school. However, everything I have done—including surviving, maintaining my spirit, and moving toward the completion of my undergraduate studies—has been against all odds. I am confident that I could be successful as a member of your first-year class.

FOR THE PAST EIGHT YEARS I have worked in the merchant marine, steadily climbing the hierarchy that exists within that organization. I realize that the merchant marine is hardly a spawning ground for MBA candidates, so perhaps a few words about the motivations behind my involvement in this unusual field would be in order. I spent most of my childhood in New England, often around the water. My family had a boat, and we often spent summers on Long Island Sound, in a community in which most activities revolved around the water. So I grew up loving boats and finding a great mystique in the sea. I spent one summer as a deckhand on a cruise boat and piloted the same boat in a subsequent summer. I chose a college which prepared me for the merchant marine because I was attracted to the idea of world travel and adventure, liked the high pay, and relished the thought of being on the sea. I also was very interested in attaining a captain's license because of the challenge it posed and because acquiring the license represented the peak achievement possible within the merchant marine. In line with my expectations, I have moved through the ranks more rapidly than most and am likely one of the youngest men now to hold the captain's license. My work involves operations, logistics, and management, and I am regarded by my captain and my men as highly capable in these areas. I have achieved all that I sought within the merchant marine and am now financially secure.

My ambitions, however, demand that I leave the merchant marine, return to land, and lead a more normal life. I now want career opportunities and challenges, as well as options in my personal life, that are unavailable to me in the merchant marine. My professional impulses are both entrepreneurial and managerial, so my projected career path will take me either into the import/export business or sports management. Having outstanding quantitative abilities and a strong interest in business, I am now eager to study for the MBA, which will give me the formal business training I currently lack.

Attending your school will provide me with a profound grasp of management principles and theories, as well as the broad perspective I will need to succeed in whatever enterprise I pursue. Your excellent reputation is a big part of your school's allure, as is your strength in the areas of financial analysis and information sciences, both of which hold particular fascination for me. Having spent the last eight years operating within a somewhat narrow environment, I am also very much looking forward to interacting with the diversity of individuals which your MBA program attracts. I expect my contacts with these persons, both students and faculty, to be highly stimulating, and I would hope to be able to add to the quality and richness of the dialogue. I have lived in your school's area during my recent leave from my ship, and I have been very impressed not only with the people in this area but also with the energy and intellectualism. It is a community of which I very much want to be a part.

The other options I have considered for next year are fairly limited. If I had to delay the start of my graduate business education, I would likely work in real estate, open a gym, or teach navigation. A fourth option would be going to Japan to teach English (I am currently studying Japanese through a university extension).

I AM A 26-YEAR-OLD WOMAN who has spent much of the past nine years engaged in such unusual activities as jumping out of airplanes, briefing Chuck Yeager (on more effective flying, of all things!), running through trenches, being a test parachutist, taking apart and then reassembling (blindfolded) a vintage M-1 rifle, earning a pilot's license, and learning how to survive behind enemy lines (including resisting interrogations and escaping captivity). All of this has occurred within the context of my time in the military, which began when I enrolled as a cadet at the Air Force Academy in Colorado Springs, Colorado.

Even then I was drawn to science, selecting biology as my major. My freshman year, when I was a lowly "doolie" (a slang derivative of the Latin word meaning "slave"), my grades suffered as I went through the traditional trials of being a first-year military student. It is a psychologically cruel and dehumanizing process (and an existence almost incomprehensible to anyone on the outside) which one must somehow endure while also meeting a full load of academic requirements. The isolation and rigidity of military life made the remaining three years a challenge as well. I frequently tell people that attending the Air Force Academy provided me the best experience of my life (in giving me discipline and showing me the stuff of which I was made) and also the worst.

At the time I graduated, I had a five-year obligation to the Air Force. Despite my continuing interest in becoming a physician, I decided first to fulfill this obligation so I would later be completely free to chart my own course. I chose to become a physiologist with the Air Force because this enabled me to combine my interest in aircraft and aerospace with my fascination with medicine. For two years I ran the hypobaric, or altitude, chamber, teaching flyers how to use their bodies to be better test pilots. During this same period I earned a master's in systems management, which I felt would help me do my job more effectively. For the past two years, I have been a human factors engineer, testing and making recommendations on equipment so its design produces optimal human performance. At night I teach scuba diving and, in line with my view that a doctor's proper role is at least partly educational, am earning a teaching credential.

With my military service scheduled to come to an end soon, it is finally possible for me to realize my long-held dream of applying to medical school. While my experience since graduating from the Air Force Academy has been highly instructive, it has reinforced my conviction that I am best suited to a career in which personal and human considerations are given highest priority. The interpersonal aspect of the profession holds great appeal for me, as does the fact that the doctor's actions have a direct and significant impact on another human's life. The constant intellectual challenge, the decision-making demands, the fast pace, and the fact that doctors can see the outcome of their work are other elements which attract me.

I know that I have a highly unconventional history for someone aspiring to become a doctor, but I also know that I have what it takes to succeed. My background has taught me many lessons, including, perhaps ironically, the value of human life and the importance of human dignity.

TWO DAYS BEFORE TAKING my LSAT exam in October, I received devastating news that turned my world upside down: My mother, who was living a continent away from me in New York, had AIDS.

Like so many other 19-year-olds, I had never given much thought to the concept of death, or to the possibility of what it might mean to lose someone so close to me. Suddenly, though, I was confronted with the very real prospect of watching helplessly as my mother battled a frightening fatal illness.

Now, 15 months later, my mother is still alive but struggling, having survived a series of extremely close brushes with death. The prognosis remains bleak, and she is not expected to live until summer. At one time she weighed only 80 pounds, down from her normal 120. I visit New York as frequently as possible in order to be near her, and find our roles seem reversed: Now I am the mother; she is the daughter.

I recount this story because my mother's circumstance has had such a profound influence on my recent life. I have done a lot of growing up very quickly. I believe I have become unusually serious and mature for someone my age. I look at many things differently. I have become very aware of life's fragility and of the importance of treating one's time and ability as the precious commodities they are. I have also been grateful to have a professional goal—to become a lawyer—that excites me and gives additional purpose to my life, especially during this difficult period when I need a focus apart from my family situation.

I am one of those fortunate people who has had a firm idea of her objectives since first starting college. I have known all along that I want to go to law school, practice law, and eventually get into politics. To corroborate my interest in a legal career, I have worked since my freshman year as an undergraduate in a series of legal jobs, normally 30 to 35 hours a week. I have worked for the L.A. city attorney (as an intern) as well as four private law firms. In these positions, I have not

---

Two days before taking my LSAT exam in October, I received devastating news that turned my world upside down: My mother, who was living a continent away from me in New York, had AIDS.

---

only been exposed to public service law but also to the workings of small, four-attorney law firms and a firm among the nation's ten largest.

As a paralegal/legal secretary I have gained a solid understanding of the legal process, from the summons and complaint through the discovery phase and to settlement or trial. I have done research and court filings, interviewed clients, sat in on depositions, and had the opportunity to become familiar with a wide range of legal documents and procedures. It is work that I love, even on the frequent occasions when it is tedious, frustrating, and anything but glamorous. I like trying to fit together pieces of a puzzle, doing the necessary analysis, facing the challenge that any case poses. I thrive on feeling productive. I find great pleasure in arguing a point, whether verbally or in writing, and am quite adept at doing this.

I believe I am well qualified to study law, having the necessary enthusiasm, energy, temperament, and commitment. Working for the city attorney heightened my awareness of, and interest in, the problems of the underserved, so public service law is the area of litigation that currently holds greatest appeal for me.

NOT EVERY DENTAL SCHOOL APPLICANT has supported himself for five-and-a-half years jousting and swordfighting in a Las Vegas show. This colorful and physically demanding work is actually just one of a number of nontraditional elements of my background. My academic history in particular is likely quite different from what you normally see. I am 26 years old and will not be completing my undergraduate work until next spring. Working each night, for a total of 42 hours a week, has forced me to structure for myself an educational schedule that has required more time in college than most spend. However, as a result, I will be emerging from my university experience with greater maturity, self-knowledge, and certainty about the professional direction I am choosing to follow than many of my peers.

Unlike many others, I did not begin college immediately after completing high school. Having no focus at that time, I chose instead to work for my uncle in the construction industry, building hotels in Las Vegas, where I grew up. I enjoyed the pay and working with my hands, but there was a void in my life and an absence of the intellectual stimulation I wanted. When I was 21, a terrible tragedy struck my family. My 19-year-old sister, who was involved with drugs, committed suicide. Her death was devastating for me and served as a wake-up call that I needed to set a meaningful course for my own life without delay. I tentatively began taking classes at a local junior college while still doing construction. Not long afterwards, though, I had the opportunity to become part of a show at a Las Vegas hotel. I was one of a dozen men selected (from 300) for this show, largely on the strength of my equestrian and fencing skills, and my size (I am 6'4" tall). Since 1990 I have worked from 5-to-midnight six (and sometimes seven) nights a week at the hotel, while also attending college. The dangers are significant and I have had my share of serious injuries, including a broken leg, a skull fracture, and a cut that required 26 stitches. Some of these injuries occasionally exerted a negative impact on my academic performance, but I have still managed to compile a very respectable record (trending upward) even with the rigorous Cell and Molecular Biology major I chose for myself.

While many around me were setting their sights on medical school, I was always drawn to the idea of entering dentistry. I enjoy working with my hands and have seen my manual dexterity through my efforts in sculpting, drawing, and building (I have remodeled my own house and built a loft within it). What I have learned during the past year, while working as a volunteer for an oral maxillofacial surgeon, has only corroborated and intensified my enthusiasm for the profession. Working with the surgeon has been an exceptional experience for me because he has allowed me to observe him in every phase of his activities, from his initial consultations with patients to the various surgeries themselves. I have watched his interactions with patients and seen how he deals with their fears and concerns. I have watched him repair broken jaws, under-bites and over-bites, and perform extractions. I am impressed with the intricacy and detailed nature of the work, the need for precision when working in such small spaces, the technicalities, challenges, and need for patience. I like the fact that dentists, oral surgeons, and orthodontists work in tandem with one another, and that there is such professionalism and collegiality within their ranks. I know that I can function well in this environment, with all of its demands, and am excited by the prospect of being able to relieve patients of their pain (be it psychological or otherwise) and help them lead happier lives. The job satisfaction expressed by virtually every dentist with whom I have spoken also appeals to me, as does the fact that dentists' schedules normally leave them time for a life outside of the office. As I am a married man who looks forward one day to raising a family, this is an important consideration.

I consider myself a well-qualified applicant who is unusually mature, grounded, determined, and committed to making an important contribution within the dental profession.

❖

ONE OF MY MOST important accomplishments occurred during my association with a restaurant chain, for which I served as director of real estate. As a relatively new corporation, this business realized that it could only grow by opening more outlets. I played a key role in helping it achieve that critical objective. I was responsible for opening nine additional stores (there were six when I joined the company), which brought company sales from just under $10 million to $27 million by the time I left.

It was my assignment to find and lease appropriate sites for our new restaurants. This was a complicated process for a number of reasons. For one, due to construction restrictions and a brisk economy, there were very few buildings available in the Greater San Francisco Bay Area. This created a landlords' market, with high rents and conditions not generally conducive to restaurant expansion. In this environment, I had to be especially resourceful and aggressive in order to do my job. Then, once I found a location that met with top management's approval, I was in charge of negotiating the deal. Such deals are complex because one is negotiating not only with landlords and attorneys but also with space planners, contractors, the city, and the health department. In the case of spaces in regional malls, I often had to work with the in-house architect and construction supervisor, as well as with the owner's design review committee. It was necessary to understand and comply with the requirements of all these various entities, although negotiation was always very much a part of the process. In my earlier experience, as a broker with a major real estate firm, I operated from a different position, representing a buyer or a seller. As real estate director for a corporation, I was suddenly an in-house principal, part of a corporate team, and it was essential that I take into account how the details of each deal would affect our business. The restaurant chain is a real estate–driven business, so my work and accomplishments were particularly vital to the company's success during this crucial phase of its development.

Another of my most important accomplishments was helping the homeless through my work for a foundation, of which I am a co-founder. This experience was remarkable because it afforded me the privilege of making a positive difference in the lives of others. The foundation achieves its goals in a number of ways. For example, for one local Family Living Center, we brought together builders and developers (who provided their services on a volunteer basis) to upgrade existing facilities, some of which were quite old and decrepit. I coordinated the work of construction teams doing the improvements. I would define the scope of the project and then assist the general contractor in subcontracting the work. I also had to go through the city permit process, which was quite unusual due to the fact that ours was a structure for the homeless.

Also, for three consecutive years, I was the operations man for a major 10K Race for the Homeless, which I originated and which was designed to raise both money and the public's consciousness of this problem. Each year about six months of planning and work would be required to set up the event, which involved many elements. Among other activities, I had to coordinate all aspects of the race with the city, police, and fire departments, establish the course and have it certified, secure the cooperation of affected neighborhood groups, and set up a complex management structure (to recruit and train volunteers as well as handle a myriad of other details). During the three years I was involved, participation in the event increased threefold and the amount of funds raised increased fourfold.

During a recent spring, I was presented with an opportunity to make a big difference in another person's life. At that time there was a six-car pileup on a highway in northern California. Heading north on the freeway just moments after this accident occurred and when the road was still open, I found my attention riveted to one particular car—crushed like an accordion—that was on fire with its driver still inside. I quickly pulled to the side of the highway, parked my car, jumped out, and ran to the car on fire. Its occupant, a teenage boy, was in a state of shock. I attempted to calm him down and then, with the help of another motorist, I used a crowbar to open the car's door. I extricated the driver from the wreckage and carried him to the side of the road before his car became totally engulfed in flames. The boy suffered a broken leg and hip, but he survived. My act was heralded in the newspapers and recognized by a citation from the highway patrol and the county in which the event occurred, but this hardly equaled the feeling I received from having saved this boy's life. Mine was a totally spontaneous and unpremeditated act, but I regard its consequence as one of my greatest accomplishments.

❖

SEVERAL YEARS AGO I WAS accepted into an MBA program in my native New Zealand. However, I decided to postpone my graduate business education until a later date.

In the intervening years, I have used my law degree and background in accounting to fill a variety of management positions with a company with annual revenues exceeding $100 million.

Working for various subsidiaries of this firm, I have been involved in reorganizing financial systems, developing and implementing new management reporting systems, negotiating union contracts, and selecting and installing computer systems, as well as, more recently, straight management troubleshooting.

My work has been challenging, varied, and educational, and in my work environment I have been granted—and become accustomed to—a high degree of autonomy. I have grown both personally and professionally. I have also learned a good deal about myself as I have functioned in so many diverse situations. I have seen that I am self-confident, aggressive, and ambitious. I have successfully navigated the uncharted waters of a number of unstructured situations by relying on what proved to be strong analytical skills and organizational abilities.

Accomplishing many different kinds of tasks over the past eight years has led me to believe that I can do much more—in fact, achieve whatever goals I set—if only I persevere and continue constantly to learn and to grow.

Others probably perceive me as a directed, capable, energetic, and athletic person. (I have competed, with considerable success, in numerous tennis and swimming contests.) They may also perceive me as someone who at times can be impatient. I have worked successfully with a wide range of individuals, but I hope that as I mature and learn I will become more of a leader.

What is most distinctive about me is that I have an international background, not only as a New Zealander but also as one who has worked extensively in Australia, Canada, Hawaii, and the continental United States. Furthermore, relying on my training as a lawyer, I have been deeply involved in litigation management. For the past three years, I have managed a number of high-rise building contract disputes involving protracted negotiations and the drafting of multiparty settlement agreements. As a result, I perhaps have a broader perspective than many others in terms of evaluating business decisions for their legal as well as economic ramifications.

❖

I FIRST BECAME INTERESTED in medicine when I entered college in 1978. When it came time to choose my major, I selected psychobiology and, accordingly, studied a curriculum with a strong emphasis on science and psychology.

Then, early in 1981, my mother became terminally ill with cancer. Although there are five other children in the family, the responsibility for caring for my mother fell to me. She needed constant care, and it was up to me to provide it.

I had to withdraw from one of my classes at school, while commuting to campus for tests in the remaining two classes (my routine with my mother made it impossible for me to attend lectures, so I had to rely heavily on my textbooks and self-study). Despite the trauma I was going through at home, I somehow managed to do well in these two classes (calculus and physics), keeping up at least part of my college career.

For four months, I spoon-fed my mother daily and helped keep her alive. I kept the entire family going, even after my mother's death, when I was emotionally and physically depleted (I had lost 15 pounds during her illness).

After it was all over and I was back on my feet, I decided I wanted to put myself back in a situation in which I could help others who were ill. I started working in the _____ hospital. . . . I also started working as a student health advocate in college, following a ten-week training period that covered diagnosis, role-playing (responding to "patients" with a wide variety of problems), first aid, and emotional concerns—all followed by extensive testing.

Caring for my mother, working at the hospital, and serving as a student health advocate—all of these experiences have not only solidified my interest in medicine but also have taught me how essential it is that physicians be sensitive to the emotional as well as physical needs of their patients. My life to date has taught me lessons that can't be learned in a classroom, lessons that—with the further academic training I hope to receive in medical school—should make me one exceptional doctor.

AT THE AGE OF 23, I AM fortunate to hold the most significant judicial role available to any student in my 25,000-member academic community. In my position, to which I was elected last spring, I enjoy the opportunity of having constant hands-on experience with the same judicial process within which every attorney works. I have studied penal law and the municipal code, researched cases, met with the parties involved in various disputes, and presided over 14 trials involving complaints that have evolved into formal charges. . . .

I serve as chairman of committees dealing with concerns as varied as community relations and the revision of the school's judicial constitution.

I began my college career on something less than a fully auspicious note. I naively chose a major not suited to my interests and wound up with my poorest grades ever. However, even as a freshman, I was showing my stripes as a leader, serving as captain of the varsity soccer team and president of my dormitory.

Since my sophomore year, there has been a significant and steady upward trend to my grades, and I have achieved about a 3.7 GPA to date. . . .

At the age of 23, I am fortunate to hold the most significant judicial role available to any student in my 25,000-member academic community.

I originally became interested in the law during my sophomore year, when I realized that my skills as a writer, speaker, and leader—as well as my powers of logic—would probably serve me well in a legal career.

All that I have done and experienced in my judicial role in college has further stimulated and reinforced my interest in the law and my determination to pursue a legal career. I believe that I have much more of an awareness of the law than the average student and a realistic perspective on what the lawyer's life entails.

❖

I GREW UP IN CIRCUMSTANCES that provide a classic example of the frequent disparity between appearance and reality. To any outsider, my family might have seemed to be enjoying the ideal upper-middle-class existence: peaceful, pretty, and privileged. In actuality, however, alcohol and domestic violence were creating an environment within our house that, for me, was both difficult and frightening.

My mother had a drinking problem, and the encounters between my father and her often escalated into violence. I spent a great deal of time trying to care for my mother, a fact of my young life that I think later on may have subliminally drawn me toward a career in medicine. Besides instilling within me a desire to help others who are ill, my experience with my mother also heightened my sensitivity to other people and the difficulties with which they sometimes must cope.

I felt some of the same sympathy while working last year with a local doctor in rural Mexico. The poverty and ignorance there, which had much to do with the parasitosis, diarrhea, and other medical problems that we saw, were very affecting. I was impressed by the difference the doctor made in these people's lives and by the appreciation that they demonstrated. I was also fascinated by my venture into an urban Mexican hospital, where I had a chance to observe Caesarean sections, treat a gunshot wound, and assist in the delivery of a child.

Complementing my Mexican experience was my three-month summer internship with an oncologist at a stateside hospital. In this position I had the opportunity to observe many physicians and a variety of surgeries, as well as doctor/patient interactions. I was also exposed to cardiology, orthopedics, and urology—among other specialties—and gained a greater awareness of the compassion and understanding that a good physician must bring to his or her work.

The experiences both here and in Mexico were inspiring to me, and I came away from them with the feeling that I could do similar work and derive great satisfaction from it.

In my personal life, I find pleasure in many different endeavors. I enjoy traveling and have visited Europe, Hong Kong, Indonesia, Tahiti, Cuba, and South America. I also enjoy expressing myself through music. Although I am not a virtuoso on any instrument, I have played the violin since the sixth grade and currently write songs on the piano and guitar. My greatest love, however, is sports, and I participate in everything from competitive tennis and volleyball to cycling and scuba diving.

I know that medical school will require that I summon all of my resources, but I have the commitment and stamina to look forward to it all. It will provide me with the best opportunity to become a productive member of society while making use of my intellectual talents in a career that I expect to be constantly challenging and fulfilling.

This business school applicant was responding to a question about important accomplishments and the role that personal commitment played.

FOR THE FIRST 20 YEARS OF my life, my activities—and self-confidence—were circumscribed by the fact that I was a chronic allergic asthmatic. I was underweight, not as strong or as well as my peers, and unable to participate normally in sports. At night I was unable to sleep without an inhaler beside my bed. I was forced to ingest heavy medication on a daily basis.

At the age of 20 I started running (slowly at first), because I discovered that this exercise—although routinely precipitating a mild asthma attack—would later enable me to sleep through the night.

Very gradually, my runs became longer. My strength improved, the severity and frequency of my attacks lessened, and soon I was able to discontinue all medication. More remarkably, after about seven years I was actually able to run 20 miles with no problem at all. This accomplishment was an enormous confidence booster as it demonstrated that a normal, healthy life was possible for me and that I could achieve anything if I set my mind to it.

Eventually it was a logical step for me to progress into competition. I found myself running in marathons and, finally, competing in triathlons. In 1983, in fact, I successfully competed in the Hawaii Ironman triathlon, arguably the most arduous and certainly the most celebrated single-day athletic endurance event.

I have assiduously pursued aerobic exercise for the past 11 years, ever since I discovered that such endeavors were finally possible for me and were the means by which I could attain physical strength and well-being. It was a long and arduous road for me—from huffing and puffing (and wheezing) my way through tentative one-mile runs to involving myself in the rigors of the triathlon—but I was determined to become fit and to stay fit.

It has made all the difference.

WHY DOES THE SHORTEST boy in the class turn out to be one of the best athletes—or the one who goes on to work for a former attorney general? As much of a cliché as overcompensating must be for someone who is small, I'm afraid I must confess to having fallen into this pattern of behavior as a consequence of my physical stature. When I was young and terribly aware of my height, I viewed sports as the best way to make up for this deficit, the best means of distinguishing myself in a world filled with boys who were taller. I became such a good skier that my parents allowed me to move away from our home in northern California so that I could attend school in Lake Tahoe and compete on the Squaw Valley race team. There, as a 13- and 14-year-old, I made the Western U.S. Junior Olympics ski team based on my success in regional races in Nevada and California. My peers eventually went on to represent the U.S. in international competition, but in order to have more time for my studies, I shifted my focus from skiing to wrestling. In wrestling I distinguished myself again, becoming captain of my high school team before a rotator cuff injury ended my participation in this sport.

In my second year of college, I turned to skiing once again as a member of my university's Alpine ski team. I have been on a race team as well, even serving as captain last year. My grades were always adequate but not stellar. Then I became an intern with a public policy think tank in Washington, D.C. For three months I spent much of my time working for former Attorney General Edwin Meese III. My job was to research material that Meese would use in his various speeches and published pieces. For this I relied on the Library of Congress and congressional and Senate sources. I also put together a 22-page summary and analysis relating to the Omnibus Drug Bill. Working in Washington was a pivotal and extraordinary experience for me in several ways. First, I gained remarkable insight into the way in which public policy is churned out and the roles which lobbyists, lawmakers, and related agencies play. Perhaps more importantly, though, I had the opportunity for the first time to test myself intellectually in a nonacademic environment. What I discovered was that I had the independence, initiative, and ingenuity necessary to fill a very responsible and challenging position. This was a great confidence booster for me; I began thinking about attending law school and returned to campus with a new enthusiasm that reflected itself in improved academic performance.

Last summer I worked 35 hours a week in my father's law office. His practice specializes in litigation involving the Public Utilities Commission, especially as related to transportation and maritime law. I did research and also had the chance to study evidence, attend hearings, and proofread both my father's pleadings and those of his adversaries. This was fascinating for me and corroborated my interest in studying law. I also became very aware of the fact that being a lawyer entails hard work, long hours, frustration, and a need for total commitment. I have this commitment because, just as I distinguished myself through sports in the past, I now want to distinguish myself through what I can accomplish intellectually as an attorney. In law I will have a long-term opportunity for work that is not only personally rewarding but which also offers me the privilege of making a difference in the lives of others.

An MBA candidate describes his leisure activities.

MY COMMUNITY ACTIVITIES HAVE been greatly circumscribed by the fact that, as an officer in the merchant marine, I have spent months at a time at sea. My leisure activities, on the other hand, have been both regular and varied, reflecting my interest in sports and exercise.

Weight lifting, which I began when I graduated from college, has transformed my lanky 150-pound frame into a somewhat more mesomorphic 170-pound physique. Previously I would have to head to the nearest gymnasium whenever my ship entered port in order to lift weights. More recently, though, I have been able to work out with weights without even leaving my ship. Largely through my own efforts, my current ship has become the first one on which I have served to feature its own designated gym.

Much of what I have done in my leisure time has depended upon my location. For example, while I was second mate on a cargo vessel stationed at a small coral atoll in the Indian Ocean, I would go ashore to jog along trails cut through lush vegetation, play racquetball, and pump iron at the local gym. I also joined a softball team that made it to the play-offs in our league.

In more recent times gymnastics has played a very important role in my life. It not only gives my body strength and definition, it also enhances my flexibility and coordination. I am currently taking classes at a local gymnastics center, where I work out on the floor, rings, parallel bars, high bar, and pommel horse.

Sports are a key element in my life because they offer camaraderie, recreation, and release. For me they have been a confidence builder as well as a consistent source of fulfillment and inner peace.

During my final year in the Ivy League, I made a grievous and totally out-of-character mistake that changed the course of my life. In the process of writing my senior thesis, I committed plagiarism.

DURING MY FINAL YEAR in the Ivy League, I made a grievous and totally out-of-character mistake that changed the course of my life. In the process of writing my senior thesis, I committed plagiarism. Even now it is impossible for me to understand fully what I did. Certainly it was an aberration, because I was someone who always had followed the rules and never had had to rely on shortcuts or cheating to succeed in academics or any other area of her life. However, in my last year in college, when I was emotionally distraught over the breakup of my parents' marriage, my behavior took an inexplicable turn. And under those circumstances I did something that was wrong and for which there is no excuse. I have spent the intervening three-and-a-half years working to remedy my error, while also immersing myself, and testing myself, in the field of law.

The consequences of my actions at my undergraduate institution were drastic. The university's disciplinary committee precluded any opportunity for me to receive my degree within the following two years and decreed that I would have to produce an entirely new thesis to be graduated at any point beyond that date. As a result, I have spent much of my time during the last 18 months researching and writing a 100-page thesis that examines the reaction of the U.S. Jewish community to refugee policy in 1938 and 1939. This effort has been undertaken while I have also been working 50 to 55 hours a week as a paralegal at a 100-attorney law firm. (I first became interested in law after working for another law firm in the summer following my junior year.) Both experiences have been important and valuable for me. Preparing the thesis has restored my confidence in my academic abilities. (I also have developed an intellectual interest in the Holocaust, at the same time that I have been deeply moved by my exposure to this very disturbing episode in our modern history.) My work in the law firm has intensified and reinforced my determination to become an attorney, while also persuading me that I have what it takes to do well in the profession.

As a paralegal I have had the opportunity to learn about many aspects of the law and to develop a very realistic concept of what it means to be an attorney. As a result I approach law school with no illusions about the profession or what it entails. I am aware of the hard work, the tedium, the deadlines, details, and frustration that are an inherent part of being a lawyer. I have also discovered that I work effectively under pressure, write well, and enjoy being a part of the law firm environment. I have managed documents for large litigation cases, summarized depositions, written up interviews, and developed databases. In the course of carrying out these and many other responsibilities, I have become excited over the prospect of preparing myself to assume a much broader role as a lawyer. I am attracted by many aspects of the law, not the least of which is the intellectual challenge it offers. I am interested in strategizing, writing briefs, and becoming familiar with whole new bodies of information for each case (in my own experience, this has included such diverse subjects as the stealth bomber, a large pharmaceutical company, and certain facets of the entertainment industry). And, if you will allow what might be a terrible cliché, I am also drawn to the law because of the opportunity it provides to help others. The firm with which I am currently associated performs a considerable amount of pro bono work, and assisting in this area is something I have found to be gratifying. I have also enjoyed volunteering at Legal Aid, where I have again been exposed to that significant segment of our population that is typically underserved by our legal system.

I am a woman who made a mistake and has worked conscientiously to make amends and set her life straight. I have seen that I can overcome setbacks and learn from my errors. I am a more compassionate and understanding person than I was four years ago, and more committed than ever to leading a life that has value. I know that I have the intellectual prowess, stamina (I am a long-distance runner and have competed in numerous 10K events), commitment, and, yes, the integrity to become an attorney who can contribute to the profession and reflect honor upon it.

SOMETIMES I LIKE TO TELL people that my father knew I wanted to be a doctor long before I did, but the truth is that the idea of becoming a physician has probably been gestating within me in some form or other since an early age. There are childhood scenes involving my father, who is a pediatrician, that are indelibly etched in my memory. When I was eight, for example, a young woman came to our door with her first baby, who she thought was dying. My father examined the infant, reassured the mother that there was no serious problem, and sent both away in a state of relief. I also remember, a few years later, being in a restaurant where a woman was choking. "Is there a doctor in the house?" someone asked. My father came forward and took the appropriate steps to help the woman in distress. In both of these instances, as well as many others through the years, I was impressed with my father's capacity to apply his knowledge and skill in a way that made such an important difference in others' lives. He seemed powerful, not in the same way as men who run companies or nations, but as someone who could provide comfort, quiet fears, touch a life, resolve a crisis.

I idolize my father and admire his commitment and contributions, but this alone would not be enough to make me want to become a doctor myself. As I matured, I had a chance to weigh other options and to take a long, hard look at myself, my capabilities, and interests. What I discovered, in time, was that medicine was indeed the most appropriate career path for me, the one best suited to me intellectually, emotionally, and otherwise. For the last four years I have worked one day a week in my father's office, which has given me the chance to interact with patients (and their mothers), observe my father at work, and better understand the dynamics of his practice. Just as when I managed a sandwich shop in high school and had to learn to deal with

I saw the delivery of babies, the treatment of gunshot wounds, hysterectomies, and a host of other procedures. I was spellbound by what I saw, and I returned to my premed studies with even greater enthusiasm and focus.

the public, within his office I have also had to be diplomatic. I have had to relate to many different types of people, often at very vulnerable moments in their lives, and do so with sensitivity and compassion.

Two summers ago I worked as an orderly in the operating room at a hospital in the Los Angeles area. I was there a minimum of 40 scheduled hours a week, and was on call each weekend. My experience at the hospital also gave me exposure to the constant pressure of emergency situations, in which there is little tolerance for error or indecision. And I was pleased to discover that I was more fascinated than repelled by the actual sight of surgery. I saw the delivery of babies, the treatment of gunshot wounds, hysterectomies, and a host of other procedures. I was spellbound by what I saw, and I returned to my premed studies with even greater enthusiasm and focus.

I have always been a very inquisitive person, as well as one who delights in taking things apart and putting them back together. I cannot help but wonder if these aspects of my personality do not somehow relate to my interest in medicine. I know for certain that I am highly attracted to the intellectual component of the profession and the fact that constant learning is such an integral part of being an effective physician. I also happen to find great pleasure in the company of other people, and I like the one-on-one facet of the physician's work.

As directed as I am in terms of my career, my life would be empty without my family, my close friends (most of whom I have known since high school), my girlfriend, and the sports in which I involve myself with great regularity. These are vital elements of my existence and help me to maintain the balance I need.

My family is very warm and loving, and I think they have nurtured in me these same qualities. Each has taken very independent and ambitious paths. My mother has recently become a lawyer; one sister is becoming a psychologist and the other sister a lawyer. My feeling about the future is that if, for any reason, I did not become a doctor, I would be wasting something—namely, my compassion, commitment, energy, and potential to contribute.

TWO YEARS AGO I FILED an EEO (Equal Employment Opportunity) suit in response to repeated episodes of apparent racial discrimination. Although the outcome was not entirely satisfactory— the offending party resigned before the case could be processed—my involvement in this action proved to be a pivotal event in my life. As an industrial hygienist with a branch of the military, I was already involved on a regular basis with the resolution of environmental problems on an advisory basis. The EEO suit heightened my awareness of the law and the extent to which legal training could enhance my effectiveness in the ongoing battle against environmental dangers.

Environmental concerns have long been one of my principal passions. This is what prompted me to secure a master's degree in public health, and this is why I have worked for nearly five years in a branch of occupational health. There it is my responsibility to recognize, evaluate, and control environmental hazards in this community of 5,000 to 8,500 employees. I interact on a daily basis with everyone from physicians, admirals, and other officers to engineers, blue-collar workers, and enlisted men. I have to keep up-to-date on a wide array of complex codes and regulations that are in a constant state of flux. My background in science, decision-making skills, judgment, ability to interpret data, and capacity for communicating with others—all of these assets are brought into play as I perform my job.

I realize that a 29-year-old woman with a background in public health perhaps does not fit the profile of the usual law school applicant. However, I have every reason to believe that I am a strong candidate for your first-year class. My 3.93 GPA in my MPH program is a clear indicator of my ability to succeed on the graduate level. Further, my success in my work has demonstrated my resourcefulness, determination, energy, and ability to manage stress and do extensive research. My interest in law is a very logical outgrowth of my commitment to the environment. Up to now I have worked to protect the health and safety of workers solely through recommendations made on an advisory basis. As an attorney I will be able to accomplish much more, to have a greater impact across the board. Very few attorneys have my background (degrees in biology, chemistry, and public health, as well as significant hands-on experience), so I will be in a unique position to do truly meaningful work and make an important contribution.

FOR THE PAST SEVEN years I have spent my summers at a camp in California, first as a camper, then as a counselor and, finally, a division head. The camp is quite remarkable in that each summer it takes in, along with its other campers, approximately 20 children with various learning disabilities, emotional disorders, and mental retardation. For two unforgettable summers I worked in the division that included these handicapped children. This proved to be one of the most extraordinary experiences in my life, as it provided me with a chance to interact closely, on a day-to-day basis, with youngsters whose courage and capacity for joy impressed me immensely. Their smiles and laughter were pure, even as they battled very significant personal difficulties for which they were not responsible. Ironically, as I worked with these children I was simultaneously fighting a small battle of my own, resisting my initial resistance to and fear of dealing with these children.

Before I got to know these youngsters, I was worried that they would detect my discomfort, catch me staring at them, misinterpret something I might say, or be hurt somehow by my actions or words. I felt that something socially unacceptable might occur. As I tend to be someone who prefers to eschew confrontation, this at first seemed a threatening possibility. The reality was that once I immersed myself in working with them, my fear of any incidents disappeared. I began relating to these children just as I would normal kids, and they sensed this and responded well. Working with these youngsters, who suffered from Down's syndrome and other serious problems, gave me a greater appreciation for my own health and a new way of relating to others who are ill.

Last summer I was back in camp as a division head. I was responsible for 79 people, including campers and staff, and had ample opportunity to test my skills as a leader, diplomat, and one who gets along well with many different types of individuals.

Deliberately putting myself in a situation that at first makes me uncomfortable is something I have done repeatedly in my life. Being scared makes me conscientious and prompts me to do a good job. In fact, I have discovered that the things I fear the most, the enterprises about which I have the most apprehension, inevitably turn out to be activities in which I excel. Medicine in general certainly represents this kind of challenge, and I would be less than candid if I did not concede that there have been moments in my premed years that I have found intimidating. However, I have also found great exhilaration in the learning process and in finding out that I was equal to any challenges that arose.

My interest in becoming a physician extends back to my childhood, although I also considered such possibilities as becoming a businessman, architect, or pilot. My father is a physician, though, so my exposure to the field of medicine was the most regular and intense, and ultimately the most inspiring. Observing my father at work and seeing his satisfaction with what he was accomplishing made a lasting impression on me. How great to do something with such benefits for others and such intrinsic reward for oneself!

For the past year I have had a chance to be a peer health counselor at my university. Working in my dorm, I provide counsel to students with a wide range of emotional and physical problems. This has given me the opportunity to be a leader and educator among my fellow students while also acquiring a little additional insight into the kinds of problems that a health professional confronts.

I have also worked for two years as a volunteer in my university hospital's emergency room, where I have been able to observe a great diversity of surgeries and the difficult conditions under which

> **I have discovered that the things I fear the most, the enterprises about which I have the most apprehension, inevitably turn out to be activities in which I excel.**

physicians often must function. I have come away from this experience with a better understanding of the sacred nature of the medical profession and the importance of the doctor's work. I have seen the need for both kindness and strength in doctors, and I have been impressed by the variety of skills that a successful physician must bring to play in his or her professional role.

AS AN UNDERGRADUATE I involved myself in a wide array of community service activities, and even now I work 40 hours a week with abused and neglected children. This impulse to serve others and put myself in situations in which I feel I am making a difference likely stems from the very difficult circumstances of my childhood, which so influenced the woman I have become.

My mother and father separated when I was six, and I was subsequently raised in a single-parent home with a mother who was an alcoholic. My father sent her $300 a month in child support (for two children), so our financial picture was also grim. (I always say my mother is a "master of ground beef" because she had to be so resourceful in stretching our food budget.) Although, fortunately, my mother was a loving parent, her drinking problem necessitated that I learn to take care of myself from a very early age. In addition to becoming independent, I immersed myself in my studies to escape the depressing realities of our family life. It was important to me that I survive and that I learn from circumstances rather than being crushed by them. My older sister did not fare so well. She dropped out of high school and, briefly, became addicted to cocaine.

By the time I began college, I was more eager than most freshmen to begin a whole new life because there was so much I wanted to put behind me. In high school I had had a full schedule of academic activities but never had an active social life. During my first semester as an undergraduate, not surprisingly, I made up for lost time. In the process, I earned the poorest grades in my academic history. After-wards I quickly got back on track scholastically, also involving myself in the first of numerous community activities, serving the homeless twice a week in a soup kitchen. Later, as service chairperson, I organized a highly successful food drive for four homeless shelters and a fundraiser for a center helping children with cancer. I also became active in a group that provides big brothers and big sisters for disadvantaged children.

I spent my junior year abroad, studying in Paris. In addition to becoming fluent in French, I eventually wrote a 30-page thesis in that language as well.

In the summer following my return, I worked as a volunteer for the National Center for Immigrants' Rights, which gave me my first experience with legal research, as well as some perspective on what lawyers do. Later I was fortunate to participate in an internship that provided me with truly extraordinary exposure to the legal system. Working 23 hours a week in a district attorney's office (in the economic crimes unit that dealt with fraud, embezzlement, and other white-collar crimes) gave me the opportunity to do extensive legal research, sit in on negotiations with defense counsel, examine and evaluate raw evidence, go to court, develop questions, and analyze the answers we would obtain. Working in the public sector offered me a large dose of reality. I was in an excellent position to observe all of the paperwork, postponements, and other frustrations that are part and parcel of practicing law. The long hours, the need for hard work and painstaking attention to detail, and the total absence of glamour were just a few aspects of the legal profession that came into sharp focus for me during my time with the DA. But rather than becoming disillusioned, I found myself becoming more interested than ever in preparing myself to become an attorney.

Since graduating I have been quite busy. I spent five weeks with my fiance in his homeland abroad, and also worked for my father, helping put together a newsletter for his property management business. For the past two months I have been a child care worker, serving as a surrogate parent and role model for seven 12- to 14-year-old boys living in a residential treatment center for abused and neglected children. The tragic and unbelievable stories to which I have been exposed in this job make me feel that my own childhood was privileged by comparison.

I am the only person in my immediate family lucky enough to have received a higher education. Now, as I look to the future, I recognize my continuing need for independence and my desire to establish myself. My life to date has prepared me for dealing with many obstacles and also shown me the resilience, strength, determination, and optimism that are so much a part of my character.

AS A DOCTOR'S SON I have been exposed to medicine all my life and independently developed a special interest in the sciences at an early age. It wasn't until my junior year in high school, however, when I saw my father bring a new child into the world, that I knew for sure that I wanted to become a doctor myself.

As I watched my father interacting with the expectant mother, trying to help her relax, then delivering her infant, I was profoundly moved: The expression "the miracle of life" assumed new meaning for me. I realized at that moment that doctors are involved in both the worst and the most wonderful moments in the lives of others and are in a unique position to help out on either type of occasion. . . .

I believe that my summer work in various medical facilities demonstrates my strong interest in and dedication to becoming a doctor, and I feel my grades indicate my aptitude in dealing with the kinds of courses that are a part of every medical school's curriculum. . . .

IN 1961, THREE YEARS BEFORE I was born in San Diego, my parents fled their native Cuba to escape Communism and the repression of Fidel Castro's regime. They spoke barely a word of English and started their new life in America with little more than the clothes on their backs.

There were no provisions in the 1960s in area schools for Spanish-speaking children, so my early years in the educational system were difficult.

Eventually, though, my academic progress enabled me to take the California Proficiency Exam and score sufficiently well that I was able to skip my senior year of high school and proceed instead to my first year of college.

Now I have become one of the state's youngest real estate brokers and, working 30 to 40 hours a week for the past two years, I have successfully built a trust fund large enough to subsidize my law school education and to allow me to spend all of my time during those three years concentrating on my studies. Up to now, my efforts in business have detracted from my performance in college; in law school, however, I am confident my grades will more accurately reflect my abilities.

During my childhood my parents were, understandably, unable to respond with much enthusiasm to my often-stated ambition of one day becoming an attorney. They were naturally more concerned with day-to-day survival than anything else and could scarcely dream of ever sending me to college, much less law school.

Just having reached the juncture in my life at which it is possible for me to apply to law school represents the fulfillment of one of my longest-held dreams. It is hard for me to forget my earliest days in school, when I could not even understand most of what my teachers were saying.

It is not surprising, I suppose, that I have a particular interest in the problems of the Hispanic community. Whatever I could do as a lawyer to help these people who are so victimized by unscrupulous businessmen, as well as their own ignorance of the law, would give me great satisfaction. . . .

❖

WHILE MY TWO YEARS OF experience in the business world have taught me substantive lessons, I approach my graduate business education with an enthusiasm, flexibility, open-mindedness, and desire to learn that I believe will serve me equally well. After securing an undergraduate degree in business, I have now had the opportunity to see how things actually work in a professional environment. I have developed a passion for business that exceeds anything I expected, as well as the conviction that—with further education and training—I have the potential to attain whatever goals I establish for myself.

I have chosen a field—finance—in which I know I can excel, principally as a result of my strong analytical abilities. One of my significant past achievements drew on just such skills. As an assignment for the real estate company for which I serve as financial analyst, I was to do a cash flow analysis for a $30-million office building that we were set to acquire. My projections for the first-year cash flow turned out—quite amazingly—to be within $10,000 of the actual figures.

The same energy and capabilities that led to my being selected as one of the top 10 (out of more than 500) business students at my undergraduate institution have made me successful in my work endeavors to date, but there is so much more I need to learn. I think the fact that I am a quick study, that I tend to assimilate new material with relative ease and speed, will help me to meet the rigorous academic challenges that your curriculum will pose. I am a detail-oriented person, but I manage to maintain a broad perspective, and I think this will be useful to me in studying for my MBA.

I am particularly interested in finance as a cornerstone in the foundation for my career in business. I want to know much more about such things as computer sciences as applied to finance (in terms of projecting financial models) and organizational behavior as it relates to working in groups.

Management consulting is my main professional goal at this point, as I like the idea of a business activity that involves extensive people contact, variety, and working regularly in different settings.

There are several reasons I am confident that I am well suited to a career in business. I am just as comfortable working with people as with numbers and greatly enjoy the personal interaction that is a part of business. I am a well-rounded individual, and I regard myself as something of a diplomat, having gracefully dealt with a number of delicate situations in my business experience. I am ambitious, motivated, persistent, and organized and have the capacity for quantitative thinking that business today demands.

When I am not working, I derive pleasure from such diverse activities as reading, traveling, and skiing. Because I also enjoy art and music, I know that I would greatly relish living in the cultural mecca that is [school's metropolitan location].

IN 1979, IN THE SOVIET city of Odessa on the Black Sea, a young man confronted a problem that would forever alter the course of his existence. This 17-year-old Jewish man, who wanted most to become a doctor, was denied the possibility of admission to medical school because of his religion. It could have been an end to a dream.

I was that man. My determination to become a physician, and my parents' support of that ambition, turned our lives upside down. We applied for a visa to leave Russia; while we waited, my parents and older brother were not allowed to work, and all of us were followed by the KGB. When we finally arrived in America in 1980, we had to make our way to Seattle without funds, friends, or command of English. My father, who is an engineer, was reduced to working as a plumber, while I began each day at 5 a.m. unloading trucks. Life was a struggle, but we were all sustained by a dream: my goal of studying to become a doctor.

Within a year of my arrival here, after attending night school to learn the language, I was able to obtain a job as an X-ray orderly at a local hospital. In this position, and later as an admitting aide, I was able over a period of three years to learn much more about American medicine. I had extensive contact with patients, doctors, nurses, and administrators and found I was able to relate well to each group. I saw

My determination to become a physician, and my parents' support of that ambition, turned our lives upside down. We applied for a visa to leave Russia; while we waited, my parents and older brother were not allowed to work, and all of us were followed by the KGB.

suffering, healing, death, and all of the other constants that make up any hospital environment. I had an opportunity to observe surgeries, from mastectomies to hysterectomies and bypasses, and to see firsthand the importance of positive doctor-patient interactions. I was fascinated by everything I saw and became more convinced than ever that I could one day make my finest contribution as a physician.

When I first entered college, I had enormous problems with English, especially scientific terminology, and my GPA was an unremarkable 2.84. However, as I mastered the language, my grades steadily improved; in fact, in the last three quarters I've earned a 3.8 GPA.

Beginning in 1984, I worked as a volunteer in the autopsy room at my university's pathology department, amassing more than 500 hours' experience. Just as the hospital provided me with a chance to observe diagnosis and treatment, the autopsy room gave me a chance to find out what goes wrong, what causes death. In that room it was possible for me to see death, smell it, touch it. I prepared organs for examination by medical students as well as assisted in autopsies and cleaning up. I was even awarded a highly sought-after scholarship in recognition of my work. . . .

I first became interested in medicine in high school, when I sat in on my brother's medical school lectures and later accompanied him on hospital rounds. My commitment to becoming a doctor, and my excitement over the prospect of being able to serve others in this capacity, is what has driven me and kept me going in the face of so many obstacles since my departure from Russia. Now, with my goal in sight and so many recent experiences reaffirming my passion for medicine, I know that all of the dedication and sacrifice have been worthwhile. I am eager to begin my medical studies, eager to meet the challenges I know they will present.

MY DECISION TO RETURN to school now and earn my MBA degree stems from my determination that I have specific needs that can best be met within the confines of a graduate business curriculum. I need more specific general management skills, a greater degree of expertise in data processing and computers, and a broader knowledge of finance (as opposed to accounting) in order to progress in my career.

Being in the business world and residing in your city, I am, of course, well aware of your reputation as one of the premier graduate business schools in the United States. The high caliber of the faculty and student population would provide me with a challenging and highly stimulating environment in which to study. The interplay of ideas would be illuminating and provocative, and the contacts I would establish within the school (and without) could only be assets to me as I continue my career.

The timing of my application to your program seems especially propitious as I will soon be leaving my firm (of my own volition) after eight productive years that have been extremely beneficial to me. I have reached the point at which there are no significant new opportunities available to me in the company that I would find exciting or rewarding. It is time to move on, and the perfect moment for me to seek to broaden the business foundation upon which the balance of my career will rest. I am eager to round out my education and fill any gaps that exist in my knowledge and understanding of business theory and the skills necessary to survive and prosper in today's fast-paced, always-changing, high-tech business world.

❖

"YOU'VE COME A LONG way, baby" is one of Madison Avenue's best-known slogans, but it also happens to reflect my own assessment of my personal growth and development during the past two years. I have gone from being a follower to being a leader, from being someone who was shy and uncertain to a person who is self-confident and even aggressive. It has been a remarkable metamorphosis, and it has changed my life.

I have learned in the classroom, but I have also learned substantive lessons in the arena of life. I have come to see that I am bright and capable, that I have as much to say and offer as anyone else, and that I have a personal warmth that attracts other people and facilitates effective communication. I have come a long way because while previously I was the person always taken by the hand, now I am the one who takes others' hands. Getting into a major university was a big confidence booster, and I viewed this as the beginning of a new period of achievement and action.

Earlier in my life things were more confused. After spending my first eight years in Southern California, I moved with my parents to Iran during a five-year period that encompassed major political turmoil. I went from being a child whose main concerns were school, sports, and TV to a youngster whose awareness of, and familiarity with, larger and more serious issues grew enormously. I returned to the United States with more sophistication and perspective, but I still didn't feel the confidence to assert myself or take chances. It wasn't until years later that I recognized the doubts that were holding me back and made a conscious decision to become a different kind of person.

Now that I have seen what I can accomplish—and have specific goals relating to a career in medicine—l believe my potential is great. I have passion and I have ability, and I believe that together these are a powerful pair. My passion for medicine developed while I was working as a volunteer at a local hospital. There I put in approximately 180 hours in the emergency and recovery rooms and discovered a particular fascination with surgery. I observed vascular surgery, an appendectomy, and orthopedic surgery, and I was deeply impressed by the skill, precision, and elegance the surgeons displayed. It is still hard for me to describe how I felt as I watched these various procedures, but I knew this was the kind of work for which I one day wanted to prepare myself.

In the Department of Hematology and Oncology at my university's hospital, I have done two years of research work in the area of osteosarcoma. This experience has instilled in me a desire to do clinical research in the area of cardiac surgery and position myself so that I might be able to develop new techniques.

Another exciting phase of my time at my university has been my involvement with the student health advocate program, which provides a liaison between students and the student health center. I was trained to do counseling, teach stress management, provide over-the-counter medication, and make referrals when appropriate. Only 40 people a year are selected for this highly competitive program, and even fewer (15) are chosen for work in my school's residence halls. I was one of those selected to work in the residence halls, and last year I was appointed recruitment coordinator for the entire student health advocate program. It has been an excellent opportunity, not only as a learning experience but also in terms of testing my stripes as a leader.

As I look toward my future in medicine, I believe one of my greatest assets will be my strength in dealing with others. I have exceptionally good instincts about other people and always seem to know how to approach them, how to talk to them. I also genuinely like people, which I think they quickly sense. I am very excited by the prospect of studying medicine and know that I have the commitment, confidence, intellectual capacity—and yes, the passion—to make mine a valuable presence within the profession.

AT THE AGE OF 33, I consider myself fortunate already to have had opportunities to work for an established corporation, for a start-up company funded by venture capitalists, and for a company of my own. Functioning in these three diverse environments has provided me with exceptional experience and a wonderful foundation upon which to build. However, in order for me to advance in my career to a degree fully commensurate with my abilities, I need the formal business training I presently lack. Your program seems totally congruent with all of my requirements not only because of its structure but also because of its pragmatic approach to teaching. As a member of the real estate industry, which is now in a slump, I find the present time most appropriate for beginning my graduate business studies. I am not as busy at work as I have often been in the past or as I expect to be in the future as my sector of the economy starts to recover. For that reason, this is the perfect moment for me to return to school and satisfy my desire to broaden my knowledge and perspective. Working in the company of so many MBA graduates impressed upon me the value of a graduate business education and made me very eager to immerse myself in a program just like yours. I want to remove the mystery that now surrounds certain subjects about which I am not knowledgeable. In addition to acquiring a much deeper understanding of finance, marketing, accounting, and other areas of business, I expect to emerge from your program with heightened credibility and the skills required to compete more effectively in today's challenging business environment. Your professors and the other businesspeople with whom I will be studying will provide an extremely stimulating and instructive experience for me, one to which I hope and expect I will be able to contribute. Further, the fact that your program includes work abroad is most appealing to me because I am intrigued by international real estate (I intend to expand my business into this sphere) and believe the opportunity to interact with foreign businessmen will be most rewarding.

❖

This MBA applicant was responding to a question concerning his childhood.

I WAS BORN 31 YEARS AGO IN Alabama, where my

father was on temporary assignment as an engineer for a company with a military aircraft contract. Our stay in the South, however, was brief, and I was still an infant when my parents returned to their native New Hampshire with my older sister and myself.

Within six years, another sister and two brothers were born. We all lived in a cozy ranch-style house on six acres. I have many pleasant memories from my time in this home, which was located at the end of a long, tree-lined dirt road. The setting was beautiful, there was space to roam, and a picturesque river was within walking distance. For a while my father continued to work for the same company, which was developing an experimental aircraft. When this company failed, though, he became a radiation health physicist for the state.

Mine was the classic small-town upbringing in many respects. The values I learned were typical for someone growing up in a community in which everyone knew his neighbors and in which family and religion played important roles. I always did well in school and was quite popular with my peers. Sports, especially baseball, were my passion from an early age. I played on a series of different baseball teams, including one that made it to a local championship. I was even part of an all-star Little League team when I was 12. My mother was eager for me to test my aptitude in other areas as well and so involved me in art, piano, guitar, and tap dancing, none of which engaged my interest as much as sports.

My parents were fairly devout Catholics and raised their children accordingly. I was an altar boy at church and spent four years at a private Catholic boys' high school. While there I attended an institute which groomed upcoming seniors for leadership positions in the student body. I exercised what I learned as a group leader at special religious events as well as in programs for retarded children.

The most memorable event of my youth was, sadly, the breakup of my parents' marriage. I will never forget the day a moving van pulled into our driveway and my mother announced to my brothers, sisters, and me that we would be relocating to another house. While I had known there were problems between my parents, this was still an unexpected and shocking development. I was a sophomore in high school, and my idyllic world was shattered. My mother, who was a registered nurse, began working again, spending long hours in a nearby hospital. My brothers, sisters, and I, who had always had the normal sibling conflicts, became much closer in the aftermath of our parents' split, and our new rapport was a source of comfort to all of us. But there were other, less positive ramifications. I did not do well in school that year, at one point skipping class for a month. Somehow I recognized on my own that I needed to be living in a more disciplined environment than existed in my mother's home and, as a result, returned to my father's house, where I lived during the balance of my high school years.

AS A NATIVE OF LOS ANGELES's inner city, where gang violence and drugs are key aspects of the landscape, I was one of the lucky few to survive childhood with spirit and ambitions intact. The poverty and despair that were all around me crushed the hopes and dreams of many of my peers; few finished high school, and even fewer went on to college. Most are now unemployed, in jail, or dead. This sad circumstance is something that is never far from my consciousness even now, as I face the exhilarating prospect of entering law school and beginning to prepare myself for the legal career that has long been a cherished goal.

I am the only member of my family ever to go to college, but at one time it seemed that this might not happen. I started my undergraduate career on a football scholarship, but a midseason gridiron injury hospitalized me and temporarily derailed my academic pursuits. Discouraged by my monthlong incapacitation, I decided to defer college and instead go to work. For two years I worked as an assistant buyer for a stereo store; for two additional years, I served as an inventory analyst for a major national toy maker. This latter job gave me the opportunity to interact regularly with both accountants and business executives, an experience which helped refuel my ambition to prepare myself for a professional career. Reentering college, I earned virtually all A's while studying economics. My success in this endeavor bolstered my confidence and helped me to cope with the challenges I faced later upon transferring to a top-rated West Coast university.

Like many law applicants, I kept an active extracurricular agenda

As a native of Los Angeles's inner city, where gang violence and drugs are key aspects of the landscape, I was one of the lucky few to survive childhood with spirit and ambitions intact. The poverty and despair that were all around me crushed the hopes and dreams of many of my peers; few finished high school, and even fewer went on to college. Most are now unemployed, in jail, or dead.

while an undergraduate. Among many diverse activities, I served as student liaison for my university's Black Alumni Association and as placement director for the Washington, D.C. Government Internship Program, as well as founding the Minority Business Association and tutoring inner-city children in math and English.

I was also fortunate to have the opportunity to do a summer internship in the nation's capital with the Legal Aid Society. Working with this group gave me a chance to sit in on depositions, accompany attorneys to court, and draft interrogatories. Moreover, I was able to play at least a small role in helping an indigent population that was unable to articulate their problems for themselves in court or afford legal counsel. I was struck by the dedication of the lawyers who staff the Legal Aid Society and by their altruistic use of their training and skills.

For the past two years I have worked (25 to 30 hours per week during school, full time in the summers) for a ten-attorney Los Angeles law firm. This experience has provided me with insights into the demands a lawyer faces and a realistic perspective on what the profession involves. I know that the effective attorney must bring many skills and talents to bear in meeting his responsibilities and that stamina, persistence, and patience can never be in short supply.

As a man who is 27 years old, I believe I would bring a maturity and seriousness of purpose to my legal studies that perhaps many younger applicants cannot offer. I have had experience in the world, I am aware of my capabilities, and I know with certainty what I want to do with the rest of my life. I have survived the mean streets of the inner city, and I have made my way in executive suites. I have a 19-year-old cousin who is an incarcerated gang member and an older cousin who has his own law firm. I know how to relate to and communicate with many different types of people, and I am interested not only in the possibility of pro bono work in my old neighborhood but also in legally serving a full spectrum of clients. I have the intellectual prowess, commitment, and enthusiasm to be an excellent lawyer, and I hope you will allow me to take the vital first step toward this goal at your School of Law.

❖

MARTIAL ARTS AND medicine. They seem worlds apart, but they both have played significant roles in my life and for reasons that are surprisingly similar. They both offer challenge, require great discipline, and necessitate a goal-oriented approach.

I first became involved with the martial arts when I was only 13 years old. At that time I began studying karate in my hometown in northern California. Even then I was a goal-oriented individual who was attracted to the step-by-step progression involved in studying karate. Within a year I had earned a brown belt (the next-to-highest ranking) and was actually serving as an instructor at the karate academy where I had learned the sport. Dedication, discipline, and physical and mental prowess were behind my success, which included being the youngest person in the area to attain the brown belt.

In college I became involved in Tae Kwon Do, which is the Korean counterpart of karate. This sport, too, requires patience, determination, and a clear mind in addition to physical strength, endurance, and agility. Within a year I had become president of my university's 80-member Tae Kwon Do club, which ranks among the top sports clubs on campus. In assuming this position I began to have the opportunity to test myself as a leader as well as an athlete.

One of the reasons I became interested in medicine is that it, too, requires a meticulous, goal-oriented approach that is very demanding. Of course, it also happens that the substance of the profession holds strong appeal for me, both in terms of the science and the potential for serving others who are in need.

Most of my exposure to the profession has occurred within the areas of surgery and emergency medicine. After first serving as an emergency medicine volunteer technician at a northern California hospital (where I had a moving experience with a young girl's death), I acquired the EMT-1A/CPR certifications and then worked as an Emergency Medical Technician-1A during a subsequent summer. This job was a fascinating, educational, and high-pressure experience that exposed me to the realities of medicine as practiced in crisis situations.

My extensive involvement with cardiothoracic surgery research over the last three years, first as a volunteer technician and currently as a staff research technician, has further fueled my desire to become a physician. I have had to rely upon my own ingenuity and problem-solving skills as well as what I have learned in the classroom, and this has been exciting. One of the more unusual aspects of my work has involved me directly in the procedure of heterotopic heart transplantation in rats. This precise and technically demanding procedure encompasses microsurgery and usually is conducted only by residents. In fact, I am the only undergraduate student doing this procedure, which has shown me the extent of both my manual dexterity and capacity for learning sophisticated techniques.

I have been fortunate enough to have had the opportunity to participate and contribute in almost every way during experiments, from administering anesthesia and performing extensive surgical preparations to analyzing the data obtained and operating monitoring and recording equipment, ventilators, and the heart-lung machine.

I am a somewhat shy individual, but I have found that within the medical environment that shyness evaporates. The opportunity to help others one-on-one is so rewarding and comfortable for me that I feel very much at ease, regardless of with whom I am working.

I think one of the particularly attractive aspects of medicine for me, especially within such specialties as internal medicine and obstetrics/gynecology, is the potential for forming close, lasting, meaningful relationships with a wide array of patients.

For me, medicine emerges as the perfect avenue for indulging my impulses to contribute, to be involved with science, and to establish important links with others at both critical and noncritical moments in their lives.

❖

FOR THE PAST 14 MONTHS I have worked in the County Clerk's Office of the local Superior Court. As a deputy clerk in this office, I have acquired a rare, hands-on knowledge of the inner workings of the legal system, learning intricacies of the judicial process unknown even to many attorneys. I have seen the difficulties and frustrations faced by both lawyers and litigants, and I have observed the many inequities that are a part of the system. Much of what I've encountered might easily have dissuaded me from seeking a career in law, but instead I find that I am more eager than ever to prepare myself to become an attorney.

Working at the Superior Court has afforded me an education I could not have obtained anywhere else. I have not only learned the dynamics of the court system but also have discovered more about both myself and the world. Most of my colleagues are poorly educated, low-income people with few good prospects for advancement in their careers. These people have, in many cases, become my friends, whose efforts to do their best, even when treated rudely, have won my respect. But working with these men and women has meant interacting with a very different group of people than that to which I am accustomed. And as a deputy clerk I also deal regularly with drug dealers, felons, auto thieves, rapists, and other criminals who represent a part of society with which I was previously unacquainted. So my position has provided me with an opportunity to see how I relate to many different types of people, also including lawyers, jurists, clerks, sheriffs, and the general public. In addition to becoming more aware of both the judicial process and people in general, I have also become more compassionate, more patient, and more diplomatic as a result of my time at the superior court. In seeing how I am capable of performing in a wide array of new situations, I have gained a heightened sense of self-confidence and a renewed enthusiasm for working within the legal arena.

What I knew about the law previously came from talking with and observing my father, who is an attorney specializing in insurance defense. He loves his work but he has never made any effort to conceal the tribulations, tedium, and disappointments that are a part of his profession. For years I have seen how hard he works, so I have never thought of the law as a glamorous field. At the same time, however, I am aware of the pleasure and feeling of personal accomplishment that can be derived from discovering a precedent, winning a point (or, even better, a case), and helping a client who has placed his trust in you. I am someone who thrives on intellectual challenge and stimulation, so this is another facet of the legal profession that holds great appeal for me. Having learned that I can interact effectively with many different types of people, the thought of also being able to serve them through a knowledge of the law is one which I find very exhilarating.

I am also excited at the prospect of continuing to lead a life that is very well rounded and filled with a diversity of activities. I grew up in a very warm, close-knit family in which sports and fitness were always a big part of our existence. My older brother, who is currently a law student, was a nationally ranked junior tennis player, and I played, even if with somewhat less distinction, on my high school team. I think this was the source of at least part of my competitiveness, which is still very much an aspect of my personality. I am a dedicated runner and have participated in at least half a dozen 10K races. I also swim, do aerobics, and spend as much time as I can with my friends, several of whom I have known all my life.

As someone who has always been very goal-oriented, I am looking forward to taking the first step toward becoming a lawyer. This is an objective I have had under consideration for several years and which my recent experiences have only reinforced.

❖

LAWYERS HAVE PLAYED an important role during three pivotal moments in my family's life and thus impressed upon me the significance of what they do. Before I describe those events, though, I must provide you with the context of the unusual circumstances under which I grew up.

Except for the fact that my parents had married and divorced each other three times, I had led a fairly normal life up until the age of ten. My father worked in a General Motors factory and provided his family with a middle-class existence that included a house and two cars. When I was ten, however, my world collapsed. My parents divorced for the fourth and final time, setting off a nasty custody battle, depleting our financial resources, and forcing my mother, brother, two younger sisters, and myself to go on welfare. (My mother had just given birth to my youngest sister and so was not able to work yet.) It was a demeaning situation that I will never forget. Our food and clothes were in limited supply. We would eat the same type of meal for two or three days in a row. Everything was a struggle, and worst of all, depending on others was humiliating.

After four years of this predicament, my mother was able to get a job cleaning houses. She often had to work nights, so it fell to me as the oldest child to care for my siblings. I became, in effect, a surrogate parent. In fact, my youngest sister was calling me "Dad" by the time she was three years old.

When I was 15, our family suffered another blow. A careless physician's faulty conclusion that my youngest sister had been molested prompted authorities to remove both my sisters from our home for several months.

Upon my sisters' return, my mother took a second, nighttime job, which placed even more responsibility on my shoulders. I had no time for a carefree teenage existence because I was too busy looking after my sisters and brother. I had concerns totally outside of the thinking of my classmates at school. This turned me into someone who was somewhat more serious and mature than many of my peers.

Somehow I still managed to do well in high school, graduating in the top five percent of my class and winding up as 1 of only 2 (of 400) seniors being accepted at my top-tiered university. Because of my family's dire financial situation, I had never dreamed that I might enjoy such an opportunity, but a generous scholarship made it all possible. My undergraduate years have been exhilarating and rewarding, and I have compiled a respectable academic record even while commuting two-and-a-half hours each day.

Law has emerged as my career choice for a number of reasons. As I indicated earlier, attorneys have been present at three key moments in my family's history. A lawyer was there during the custody battle that my mother won, a lawyer provided the counsel that led to my sisters' being returned to us (he recommended that a second doctor examine them, thus negating the molestation charge), and a lawyer helped my mother through a critical period when she had gone deeply into debt (not surprising for a woman raising four children on $8,000 a year).

As I move toward the completion of my undergraduate days, I feel very grateful for the blessing of the education I have received. My parents, both Peruvian immigrants, never went beyond high school. While I enjoyed all the benefits of my university experience, my mother was still cleaning other people's toilets in order to try to make ends meet. As a lawyer, I will be in a position to achieve some measure of financial stability and help out my mother. I will also be able to give something back to others. (I speak Spanish, which should be an asset to me in Southern California.) Majoring in history has refined my research skills and prompted me to recognize that I will likely enjoy studying precedents and other aspects of the legal process. I enjoy writing, relate well to others, and, not surprisingly, feel a special compassion for those who are disadvantaged. Last year, in fact, I spent six months doing volunteer work at the Interfaith Hunger Coalition, which provides leads to individuals who are seeking food.

Considering my background, I believe I have already come a long way in my life and have demonstrated that I am both a survivor and a hard worker.

❖

I AM A VERY PASSIONATE, driven, and intense individual who thrives on both challenge and competition. Although I did not distinguish myself academically as an undergraduate (distracted as I was by a difficult outside work schedule), I have had many opportunities in the intervening years to test myself in demanding situations and see that I am bright and highly capable. Indeed, I have more than held my own while working in sophisticated settings with MBA graduates and other business people with substantially more experience and training than I. Fortunately, I am a quick study and am able to grasp new ideas quite easily. I have strong interpersonal and communication skills, and I am an adept negotiator who now has considerable experience in this area. I tend to lead by example rather than charisma, although I am personable and seem to inspire loyalty in those who work with me. I have discovered in the professional world that I am a principled person whose integrity leads me, when faced with difficult decisions, to do the right thing, keeping in mind how my actions impact other people. I have a social conscience because, as a first-generation American, I am very aware of the struggles of my mother's family, which came here from El Salvador, where human rights have little significance.

In terms of developing myself, I want to learn to be more persuasive. Although I communicate well and function with great effectiveness as a negotiator, I believe that I need to become more capable of bringing others to my point of view so that a consensus can be established. I also would like to develop further my ability to work as part of a team.

I believe the most distinctive thing about me is that I eagerly take on challenges that other people are reluctant to assume. I like being challenged, being pushed to be resourceful, being forced to go beyond what I might have previously considered my limits. Agreeing to handle the complex task of running a major 10K race for the homeless is a perfect example of this. Similarly, I was typically the broker who consented to accept difficult institutional clients with whom others were loath to work.

DURING MY FRESHMAN year, I was seriously ill with what was eventually diagnosed as mononucleosis. Extreme fatigue, swollen glands, and such secondary problems as persistent colds and sore throats were among the symptoms from which I suffered.

Because the mononucleosis was not correctly diagnosed and proper treatment begun until the second half of the school year, I went through many months of feeling terrible. The consequences for my academic performance were devastating; I earned the poorest grades of my life during the prolonged period of my illness. The only up side to this episode was that I suddenly realized, much more than most teenagers ever do, that good health is a very precious commodity and one that can never be taken for granted. In addition, I gained a very deep appreciation of the role physicians can play in improving their patients' lives.

With this in mind, and considering my long-demonstrated proficiency in the sciences, it is probably not surprising that the following school year I decided to follow a premed curriculum, with biology as my major. I found myself taking the most difficult, challenging courses I had ever faced, but I also found myself more exhilarated and excited about my studies than ever before. I enjoyed the entire premed environment, including not only the learning and intellectual stimulation but also the competitiveness that is such a big part of it. I have always considered myself a problem solver, and the premed curriculum provided me with a plenitude of opportunities for defining and solving a wide variety of problems.

When I completed my undergraduate work, I chose a somewhat unconventional course for someone intent on becoming a doctor.

Rather than heading straight for medical school, I did something entirely different. After taking a physics course that I had not been able to work into my schedule previously, I moved to Jackson Hole, Wyoming, for five months to attempt to become an expert skier. Always an above-average skier, it was my goal to become a great skier. I knew that once I entered medical school and, later, the medical profession, I would never have the time to realize this objective. So I took a part-time job in Jackson Hole (first as a resort cashier, then as manager of a concession stand) to support myself while I took lessons and skied furiously in the pursuit of excellence. The results that I achieved were outstanding and were a great boost to my self-confidence, especially since Jackson Hole offers some of the biggest challenges in skiing. The time I spent in Wyoming was very beneficial for me in other ways as well because it gave me a chance to immerse myself in a totally different environment and reassess my professional objectives. I came away from Jackson Hole not only feeling refreshed and recharged, but also with a renewed sense of enthusiasm about my plans to attend medical school and become a doctor.

MY INTEREST IN SCIENCE dates back to my years in high school, where I excelled in physics, chemistry, and math. When I was a senior, I took a first-year calculus course at a local college (such an advanced-level class was not available in high school) and earned an A. It seemed only logical that I pursue a career in electrical engineering.

When I began my undergraduate career, I had the opportunity to be exposed to the full range of engineering courses, all of which tended to reinforce and solidify my intense interest in engineering. I've also had the opportunity to study a number of subjects in the humanities, and they have been both enjoyable and enlightening, providing me with a new and different perspective on the world in which we live.

In the realm of engineering, I have developed a special interest in the field of laser technology and have even been taking a graduate course in quantum electronics. Among the 25 or so students in the course, I am the sole undergraduate. Another particular interest of mine is electromagnetics, and last summer, when I was a technical assistant at a world-famous local lab, I learned about its many practical applications, especially in relation to microstrip and antenna design. Management at this lab was sufficiently impressed with my work to ask that I return when I graduate. Of course, my plans following completion of my current studies are to move directly into graduate work toward my master's in science. After I earn my master's degree, I intend to start work on my Ph.D. in electrical engineering. Later I would like to work in the area of research and development for private industry. It is in R & D that I believe I can make the greatest contribution, utilizing my theoretical background and creativity as a scientist.

I am highly aware of the superb reputation of your school, and my conversations with several of your alumni have served to deepen my interest in attending. I know that, in addition to your excellent faculty, your computer facilities are among the best in the state. I hope you will give me the privilege of continuing my studies at your fine institution.

HAVING MAJORED IN literary studies (world literature) as an undergraduate, I would now like to concentrate on English and American literature.

I am especially interested in nineteenth-century literature, women's literature, Anglo-Saxon poetry, and folklore and folk literature. My personal literary projects have involved some combination of these subjects. For the oral section of my comprehensive exams, I specialized in nineteenth-century novels by and about women. The relationship between "high" and folk literature became the subject for my honors essay, which examined Toni Morrison's use of classical, biblical, African, and Afro-American folk tradition in her novel. I plan to work further on this essay, treating Morrison's other novels and perhaps preparing a paper suitable for publication.

In my studies toward a doctoral degree, I hope to examine more closely the relationship between high and folk literature. My junior year and private studies of Anglo-Saxon language and literature have caused me to consider the question of where the divisions between folklore, folk literature, and high literature lie. Should I attend your school, I would like to resume my studies of Anglo-Saxon poetry, with special attention to its folk elements.

Writing poetry also figures prominently in my academic and professional goals. I have just begun submitting to the smaller journals with some success and am gradually building a working manuscript for a collection. The dominant theme of this collection relies on poems that draw from classical, biblical, and folk traditions, as well as everyday experience, in order to celebrate the process of giving and taking life, whether literal or figurative. My poetry both draws from and influences my academic studies. Much of what I read and study finds a place in my creative work as subject. At the same time, I study the art of literature by taking part in the creative process, experimenting with the tools used by other authors in the past.

In terms of a career, I see myself teaching literature, writing criticism, and going into editing or publishing poetry. Doctoral studies would be valuable to me in several ways. First, your teaching assistantship program would provide me with the practical teaching experience I am eager to acquire. Further, earning a Ph.D. in English and American literature would advance my other two career goals by adding to my skills, both critical and creative, in working with language. Ultimately, however, I see the Ph.D. as an end in itself, as well as a professional stepping-stone; I enjoy studying literature for its own sake and would like to continue my studies on the level demanded by the Ph.D. program.

❖

I ORIGINALLY BECAME INTERESTED in the health care field at a very early age because my mother was a nurse and I spent considerable time in my childhood observing her at work. I was attracted to the idea of helping people with physical problems, although I had no thought about any specific specialty. However, in time physical therapy became the logical focus of my attention for a number of reasons. For one, I have memories from a very young age of my grandfather in Czechoslovakia, disabled by a stroke, his problems unmitigated by any attempts at physical therapy. I will never forget the devastating consequences of this. Conversely, I clearly recall suffering from scoliosis when I was 6 years old and having physical therapy permanently relieve me of the problem. My grandmother, too, was helped by physical therapy after suffering a hip fracture when she was 89 years old. She is 95 now and still quite active. So, even within my own family, I have seen the benefits of physical therapy in a dramatic way and how it can positively change an individual's life. I have been impressed, too, by the fact that physical therapy provides a non-invasive means of treatment that can yield such long-lasting results.

Until two-and-a-half years ago, my professional background was in the area of mechanical engineering. After a while, though, I decided I wanted finally to make the move into the medical field. Physical therapy represents the perfect choice, a career with definite parallels to the work I have done previously; within it I will be able to draw upon my knowledge and understanding of mechanics and motion, and also use my analytical abilities to resolve challenging clinical problems. Four months as a volunteer and two-and-a-half years as a physical therapy aide have only served to corroborate and enhance my interest in the profession.

As far as my professional goals are concerned, I want to specialize in geriatrics and neurological disorders, and come to be known for my professionalism, effectiveness, and compassion. Currently I work for a hospital group with separate in-patient and outpatient facilities. This has given me a chance to observe patients over long periods of rehabilitation and develop rewarding relationships. It is my goal to do the same once I become a registered physical therapist. I hope to be working then in an acute care hospital with an outpatient facility and participate in research that furthers growth in the profession.

I HAVE BEEN PLANNING a career in geological sciences for several years, but as an undergraduate I concentrated on getting a solid background in math and science. After graduation, I took a job to allow myself time to thoroughly think through my plans and to expose myself to a variety of work situations. This strategy has been very valuable to me in rounding out my career plans.

During the past 18 months I have had firsthand experience with computers in a wide array of business applications. This has stimulated me to think about ways in which computers could be used for scientific research. One idea that particularly fascinates me is mathematical modeling of natural systems, and I think those kinds of techniques could be put to good use in geological science. I have always enjoyed and been strong in areas that require logical, analytical thought, and I am anxious to combine my interest in earth science with my knowledge of, and aptitude for, computer-related work. There are several specific areas that I have already studied that I think would lend themselves to research based on computing techniques, including mineral phase relations in igneous petrology and several topics in structural geology.

I have had both lecture/lab and field courses in structural geology, as well as a short module dealing with plate tectonics, and I am very interested in the whole area. I would like to explore structural geology and tectonics further at the graduate level. I am also interested in learning more about geophysics. I plan to focus on all these areas in graduate school while at the same time continuing to build up my overall knowledge of geology.

My ultimate academic goal is to earn a Ph.D., but enrolling first in a master's program will enable me to explore my various interests and make a more informed decision about which specific discipline I will want to study in depth.

As far as long-term plans, I hope to get a position at a university or other institution where I can indulge my primary impulse, which is to be involved in scientific research, and also try my hand at teaching.

❖

MY LONGTIME FASCINATION with politics and international affairs is reflected in my participation, starting in high school, in activities such as student council, school board meetings, Vietnam war protests, the McCarthy campaign, and the grape boycott. As each new cause came along, I was always ready to go to Washington or the state capital to wave a sign or chant slogans. Although I look back on these activities today with some chagrin, I realize they did help me to develop, at an early age, a sense of concern for social and political issues and a genuine desire to play a role.

As an undergraduate, I was more interested in social than academic development. During my last two years, I became involved with drugs and alcohol and devoted little time to my studies, doing only as much as was necessary to maintain a B average. After graduation my drug use became progressively worse; without the motivation or ability to look for a career job, I worked for a time in a factory and then, for three years, as a cab driver in New York City.

In 1980 I finally "hit bottom" and became willing to accept help. I joined both Alcoholics Anonymous and Narcotics Anonymous, and for the next several years the primary business of my life was recovery. Although I had several "slips" in the beginning, I have now enjoyed nearly seven years of complete freedom from drug and alcohol use. I mention my bout with addiction because I think it is important in answering two issues that presumably will be of concern to the admissions committee: my lackluster undergraduate record and the fact that I have waited until the age of 34 to begin preparing academically for a career in public policy. It would be an oversimplification to call addiction the cause for either of these things; rather I would say it was the most obvious manifestation of an underlying immaturity that characterized my postadolescent years. More importantly, the discipline of recovery has had a significant impact on my overall emotional growth.

During the last years of my addiction I was completely oblivious to the world around me. Until 1983 I didn't even realize that there had been a revolution in Nicaragua or that one was going on in El Salvador. Then I rejoined the Quaker Meeting, in which I had been raised as a child, and quickly gravitated to its Peace and Social Order Committee. They were just then initiating a project to help refugees from Central America, and I joined enthusiastically in the work. I began reading about Central America and, later, teaching myself Spanish. I got to know refugees who were victims of poverty and oppression, became more grateful for my own economic and educational advantages, and developed a strong desire to give something back by working to provide opportunities to those who have not been so lucky.

In 1986 I went to Nicaragua to pick coffee for two weeks. This trip changed my whole outlook on both the United States and the underdeveloped world. The combination of living for two weeks amid poverty and engaging in long political discussions with my fellow coffee pickers, including several well-educated professionals who held views significantly to the left of mine, profoundly shook my world view. I came back humbled, aware of how little I knew about the world

I joined both Alcoholics Anonymous and Narcotics Anonymous, and for the next several years the primary business of my life was recovery. Although I had several "slips" in the beginning, I have now enjoyed nearly seven years of complete freedom from drug and alcohol use.

and eager to learn more. I began raiding the public library for everything I could find on the Third World and started subscribing to a wide variety of periodicals, from scholarly journals such as *Foreign Affairs* and *Asian Survey* to obscure newsletters such as *Through Our Eyes* (published by U.S. citizens living in Nicaragua).

Over the intervening two years, my interest has gradually focused on economics. I have come to realize that economic development (including equitable distribution of wealth) is the key to peace and social justice, both at home and in the Third World. I didn't study economics in college and have found it difficult to understand the economic issues that are at the heart of many policy decisions. At the same time, though, I am fascinated by the subject. Given my belief that basic economic needs are among the most fundamental of human rights, how can society best go about providing for them? Although I call myself an idealist, I'm convinced that true idealism must be pragmatic. I am not impressed, for example, by simplistic formulations that require people to be better than they are. As a Quaker I believe that the means are inseparable from the end; as an American I believe that democracy and freedom of expression are essential elements of a just society, though I'm not wedded to the idea that our version of democracy is the only legitimate one.

Although I have carved out a comfortable niche in my present job, with a responsible position and a good salary, I have become increasingly dissatisfied with the prospect of a career in business

The combination of living for two weeks amid poverty and engaging in long political discussions with my fellow coffee pickers, including several well-educated professionals who held views significantly to the left of mine, profoundly shook my world view.

applications programming. More and more of my time and energy is now being absorbed by community activities. After getting my master's in public administration, I would like to work in the area of economic development in the Third World, particularly Latin America. The setting might be a private (possibly church-based) development agency, the UN, the OAS, one of the multilateral development banks, or a government agency. What I need from graduate school is the academic foundation for such a career. What I offer in return is a perspective that comes from significant involvement in policy issues at the grass roots level, where they originate and ultimately must be resolved.

❖

This MBA applicant was discussing indicators of leadership, innovation, and professional potential.

I BELIEVE I HAVE been showing my stripes as a leader ever since my days as captain of a high school volleyball team that was ranked fifth in the state of California. In college I again served as captain of the volleyball team, this one ranked in the Top 10 nationally. Leading one of the country's most outstanding NCAA Division 1 teams involved significant challenge and responsibility, both in and away from competition. I had to recruit new talent to assure continuity in the success of our team, and fill various PR functions necessary to generate interest in, and funds for, the team. I had to be able to communicate effectively not only with players but also with the coaching staff, referees, and the school administration. I had to motivate, stay cool under pressure, instill discipline, and lead by example, and was successful in each of these endeavors.

More recently I have been playing semi-pro beach volleyball and even had the opportunity to make a highly significant contribution to the sport. A friend and I laid the groundwork for the establishment of an association which represents the interests of approximately 100 players. Since the association was begun, prize money on the players' tour has gone from $50,000 to $1 million, with control shifting from the promoters to the players. I also have been running the computer ranking system, which I personally devised and implemented. This system—along with the association itself—has revolutionized volleyball for the players and given the sport a new vitality. My achievement in creating this system reflects not only my leadership but also my imagination and proficiency in dealing with computers, which I have cultivated during the past six years.

I have been able to draw upon my creativity and knowledge of computers in my work environment as well. In addition to developing the computer-based solution to the merchandise problem described elsewhere, I have also utilized my computer skills in another important project at the women's clothing store chain where I work. Because expansion is now such a key element of its business plan, I was asked to devise for the company a computer program that would assess the profit potential of prospective new stores. Accordingly, I developed a program to project cash flow and the return on investment for the first ten years of each new store's operation. This program gained instant approval from top management and is now being used on a regular basis. My role in this vital, ongoing process of opening new stores is indicative of my professional potential and has afforded me the opportunity of interacting regularly with key executives at our own company as well as our parent. My contacts with these individuals have demonstrated to me my ability to function effectively in the milieu of high-level management and to be taken seriously by business people of considerable experience, stature, and sophistication.

MY DECISION TO WORK in the nonprofit sector, with developmentally disabled individuals who require much patience and attention, reflects the fact that my principal concerns have revolved around issues other than money. I knew from the moment I completed my undergraduate work that I wanted to place myself in a professional environment in which I could make a positive difference in other people's lives, and do work that contributed somehow to society at large. At the nonprofit organization where I work, I have been able to accomplish just that. Our clients, whose employment and other opportunities were previously highly limited, find through our organization not just work but a new sense of purpose and worthiness. These are good people whom life has dealt a difficult hand. It is impossible not to feel a sense of compassion for their plight. The fact that we are able to provide them with a place to come every day, a salary, a new group of friends, and the feeling that they are capable of doing meaningful work makes all of the challenges of my job worthwhile. Our society is filled with people who need our help; if I can continue to merge my concerns and my managerial skills in a way that yields positive results, I will be pleased. I am committed to my work because I believe it is important. Just as I was dedicated to sports and, later, scholarship at earlier times in my life, now I am dedicated to my career. Such dedication is perhaps especially necessary within the nonprofit sector, where personal financial reward is clearly not a motivation. One's commitment to the cause, to the work, is crucial because there are constant problems and challenges, and resources tend to be limited.

This very limit to financial resources, which is the bane of the existence of so many nonprofit organizations, is exactly the reason that creativity is essential for managerial success in this sector. At the nonprofit where I work, for instance, I have had to be creative in numerous different ways, from developing new programs (as with one involving recycling) and generating community support, to creating new work methods and schedules.

Being a part of diverse teams has been a constant part of my work experience. In addition to working in a cooperative way with developmentally disabled individuals on a daily basis—with all of the sensitivity, understanding, and patience that this requires—I have also interacted regularly with our own upper management, volunteers, city officials who oversee municipal contracts with our organization, state government officials, and private industry. I quickly came to realize how many different entities are involved in organizations of any size, especially one like ours. The ability to work with and relate well to all of these different groups, each of which has its own values and agendas, is critical.

If I had any question about whether I was a leader coming out of college, that concern was forever put to rest once I joined the nonprofit organization. For there I have repeatedly had to draw upon a variety of leadership skills in order to do my job successfully. I have seen that I work well with many different kinds of people, am able to think creatively, negotiate effectively whether with workers or city officials, overcome constant challenges, meet deadlines, and establish and realize goals.

PART III:

THE INSIDE PERSPECTIVE

Advice from Admissions Representatives of Leading Graduate and Professional Schools

> **Jill Fadule**
> Director of Admissions
> Harvard Business School

OUR CRITERIA IN TRYING to decide who to admit are: strong evidence of academic ability, for which the transcripts, recommendations, and the GMATs are helpful; evidence of the candidates taking on leadership and management positions either in their full-time paid work, their community work, or their extracurricular work when they were in school; and the potential for future leadership, which we look for in terms of certain personal qualities and characteristics that we care about. I'm referring to things like honesty, integrity, maturity, commitment to others, and motivation—some of the things that you might expect and then also some things maybe not so expected like self-awareness, self-esteem, empathy, willingness to take risks, willingness to deal with ambiguity. These are things that we think have helped our graduates and some other business leaders to be successful.

We don't ever ask applicants for a single personal statement or summary, or ask them to tell us about themselves in a general way; we really are asking about specific events, failures or accomplishments, times when they've had the opportunity to lead, or people who have influenced them.

What I would love to have people do in preparing their essays is to do a great deal of self-assessment and reflection on their lives and on what's important to them because the most important thing to us is to get a very candid and real sense of the person. I think people do themselves a real disservice if they think too much about what they think Harvard would like to hear, or if they think about what might have been successful in the past in being admitted to Harvard. It's a lot more helpful to us and, in the long run, to them if they are very candid and really approach the questions as though they are answering them to a close colleague because we want to get a feel for the whole person; we don't want to know just what they think we want to know. Sometimes people assume that since they are applying to business school, they need to focus all of their essays on their long-term interest in business when, in fact, there are other things that were very important to them that didn't actually occur in their business life [but a discussion of which] would provide an opportunity to show the qualities that we care about. So, in not telling us about these things, they really do themselves a disservice.

Try to answer questions as you would to a close colleague. Try to allow yourself a full week away from the essays, then go back and look at them again before sending them in. We always get calls from people who finished their essays, pushed "Print" and [later] wished they had [taken] more time to make them even better. So leave yourself some time to reflect on the essays and then ask yourself, "Is this a true picture of me? If someone had never known me before, would they really know me after reading these essays?" Sometimes people get too caught up in the heat of the moment and they don't allow themselves that type of time. Take the essays seriously.

Mistakes? People assume that we look at their title and the fact that [for example] they've been promoted faster than their peers and assume that, for them, the essays [then] aren't as important because of what their recommenders will say about them or what their title or salary may say about them. They think, "This fast promotion is at least going to get me an interview and then I can use that time to really differentiate myself." But the fact is that we use the written application to decide who gets to interview. Everyone, no matter how successful they've been in their careers, needs to set aside the time to prepare the essays carefully and thoughtfully; they should not assume we care so much about the position they've achieved that we won't care about the content of their essays.

Another problem is with people who give us sort of a boilerplate set of responses; someone has told them, "When I was applying to Harvard, I talked about these three things," so they talk about those three things (when they really weren't that important to them), so we don't get the full picture of the candidate.

We are doing an increasing number of interviews. Years ago it was some tiny number like 40, but last year we did 1,300 interviews [out of an application pool of 8,000]. We first review the application as an admissions board and then vote on whether the candidate is a strong one we think would be worthwhile to interview. So it's a positive sign to be asked for an interview; not everyone gets asked. However, not everyone invited to interview gets in, as I think most people

> **Everyone, no matter how successful they've been in their careers, needs to set aside the time to prepare the essays carefully and thoughtfully; they should not assume we care so much about the position they've achieved that we won't care about the content of their essays.**

understand. Last year about 55 percent of the people we interviewed were admitted, but historically it's been closer to 50 percent of the people we interview who end up getting admitted. This year greater than 80 percent of the admitted students have had an interview as part of their admissions process.

[In continuing to pose a large number of questions] we're really trying to get a full picture of the candidate and understand who this person is. The GMAT isn't going to help us with that, so having it [again, after 10 years when it was not required] doesn't translate into a reduction in [the number of] essays because the GMAT isn't giving us information about who the person is, what that person's experiences have been working with other people, what the person has learned from his or her failures.

The number of readers does vary by the quality of the application itself. There are three or four readers usually, but fewer for some of the less competitive candidates. Many of the readers are graduates of our program—like I am myself.

Stephen Christakos
Former Director of Admissions
J. L. Kellogg Graduate School of
Management (Northwestern University)

I'M GOING TO TALK MOSTLY about one essay that is fairly common among schools, the one that deals with why you're applying to a certain professional program and school and where you're headed careerwise. In this we're looking for students who show good self-awareness and a good sense of career awareness. We want students whose motivation for pursuing an MBA is clear, who seem to understand well what the Kellogg program offers, and who make rational arguments about why it's a good match for them. Applicants need to convey strongly why they're going to give up a job and spend the time and money to attend, and they need to be able to address where they're headed post-MBA.

I was admissions director at Wharton prior to Kellogg and at the University of Virginia's Darden School prior to that, so I'm kind of a unique person in this business in that I've been around and been a director of three top-tiered MBA programs. My advice to the applicant is to be honest in your essays, lay it out, and be as specific as you can, but don't try to second-guess what the admissions committee wants to hear. Keep it concise and to the point, and answer the question. You want particularly to avoid what I call the "grab-bag phenomenon": throwing into an essay everything you think the admissions people might want to hear. At the same time, don't prejudge what the committee wants and therefore leave out important material. We do care about what we call the "sparkle quotient" in our classes; we want to know what students do with their free time, what makes them tick outside of work hours, and whether they've demonstrated the ability to work with and help others.

I always encourage students to get applications for all schools in which they have an interest and start working on all of them simultaneously. If you instead finish one at a time and mail it off, you do not have the chance to revise an essay when you find a better way to approach a topic in a later application. Have your interview prior to or during the essay-writing process. It might help you to visit, talk through your motivation, talk through your accomplishments, and get to know the school's culture a bit before you finalize these essays. You learn a lot about yourself when you are interviewed. I often get application addendums or letters from candidates who have visited

> **We want to know what students do with their free time, what makes them tick outside of work hours, and whether they've demonstrated the ability to work with and help others.**

and want to change an essay afterward.

Be careful on some of the gimmicky things: addendums to applications, videotapes, samples of your work (remember the old adage: "the thicker the file, the thicker the candidate"). If it's appropriate to send something in—if it's going to support a major accomplishment you've talked about—that's fine, but sometimes I think it's done just as an attention-grabbing gimmick and doesn't really shed more light on the applicant and his or her qualifications.

Each file is read by a minimum of three people: a student member of the committee reads it first, a staff member next, and then I review every file (there were 9,500 in a recent two-year period). If there's not consensus among the three, the file automatically goes to a fourth and occasionally even a fifth reader. It's a very thorough and very fair process.

For more than five years now, we've required an interview (96 percent of the applicants are able to comply); we've got 850 alumni in 31 countries now interviewing for us. The interview is often the first thing we have. And even if we have a file before the interview, we will not look at it because you tend to get biased. With a clean slate, we can get a sense of how you present yourself in person (that's important for a manager), how mature you are, how focused you are, your sense of humor, and how you verbalize a lot of the things we're going to be asking for later in writing.

Bob Alig
Director of MBA Admissions and
Financial Aid
The Wharton School
(University of Pennsylvania)

THE MOST IMPORTANT THING [for me to do] is communicate what we're not looking for, which is to say that there is no magic formula for admission, there are no right answers. I think it's absolutely critical that prospective students avoid the trap of trying to tell us what they think we want to hear. I am attempting to get to know the prospective student as an individual. I want the prospective student to provide me with sufficient context for an appropriate evaluation by the admissions committee. In addition, I'm looking for perspective on an individual student's decision-making process throughout his or her life, with a particular emphasis on the professional development to date.

What I oftentimes see is that people use the essays to focus on lots of things that are extraneous to them, such as their individual work experience; what they do becomes more of a focus than who they are. I am really struggling to get to know the applicants as people and I frankly don't want to hear about the minutiae of their work. I want to hear why they chose to do what they do, why they chose to go to school where they did, what they value about those individual experiences and the impact of these experiences on their development as people. This process of self-examination and subsequently sharing it with the admissions committee can make prospective students feel vulnerable, and I think that's why the essays become difficult. [However] I think students should take a certain degree of comfort if this process is difficult for them [because it means] they're probably on the right track. The decision-making processes are so important because they illustrate who this person is. Oftentimes I hear "Well, I went to Berkeley as an undergrad, I studied engineering, I got a 3.6 GPA, I was president of my sorority, and I work for Coopers & Lybrand. How do I distinguish myself in your applicant pool?" Well, giving me those data points from a resume will not distinguish them in my applicant pool at all, but [what will is] telling me why they chose to go to Berkeley, what they value about their experience at Coopers & Lybrand, how these individual experiences have impacted them, and also telling me about their decision-making process to attend an MBA program. Only one person in my applicant pool can answer those questions just the way this person can. An essay that gives me this type of perspective is automatically going to enable this person to stand out in my applicant pool even if their resume looks somewhat similar to others'.

I think sometimes there's an apprehension on the part of our applicants [because] they've never overcome some life-threatening disease or some other huge obstacle in their life, personal or otherwise. These people shouldn't be apprehensive; an applicant's response to ordinary life events, like adjusting to college or a new work environment, dealing with being terminated at work, or shifting to a new department as a result of downsizing, can be very compelling to the admissions committee. An applicant doesn't need to have overcome monumental obstacles in order for me to be very excited about a person's candidacy and what he's communicating to me. I want perspective on successes and failures and how you have handled both throughout your life.

As far as mistakes, often we see essays that are somewhat generic and look like they have been cut and pasted from the essay questions from other schools; they just don't show a whole lot of creativity or originality, and that's a problem. Some students fail to communicate their message succinctly. This is important because they're trying to communicate a message and extraneous information can dilute or diminish that message. I want to see some passion and sincerity and I want these essays to come off the page a little bit, but I don't want the applicants to be something they're not. Some people think the way to stand out is to infuse their essays with humor; if that's not your usual approach to communication, then it shouldn't be your approach in your essays because they should be a reflection of who you are. I also have to mention grammar and spelling [as potential mistakes]. And, frankly, another caution would have to be that spell-check does not pull the name of other MBA programs out of essays [intended for Wharton]. The application is a representation of the student and his or her commitment to our program, and the only one over which students have absolute control, so they should really take ownership of it and take some comfort that this is something they can control. They can't control the tone of the recommendations; they might have an interview with someone who's not having a good day; they might not be a good standardized test taker; they might have had a couple of rocky academic semesters [as an] undergrad—lots of things they can't control or change at this point. But the essays are theirs and theirs alone. So I do put a certain premium on how they reflect on the individual. I'm looking for that passion and sincerity and for a human quality to emerge. I'm reading thousands of them—and I do read every single word, so when I see one that really does demonstrate a lot of thought and provides me with valuable personal and professional perspective on an individual, it does stand out for me. They should spend a lot of time thinking about their essays and the message about themselves they are trying to communicate to the admissions committee.

Advice? They should take ownership of the essays and savor the opportunity to tell us a story that only they can tell us. But I also think they need to take some comfort in the fact that we do not admit superhumans; there are no superhumans out there. We admit students for a variety of reasons. Every student we admit has certain deficiencies and shortcomings in his or her candidacy, so you want to emphasize your strengths, minimize your weaknesses, and make it abundantly apparent to me that you're going to make this learning community and the MBA experience stronger by being here. This is because, frankly, 80 percent of the people who apply to very competitive, top-tier MBA programs can handle the workload. So the question often becomes not "Can the student make it here?" but [rather] "How is the student going to contribute here, how is he going to make us stronger or make an imprint on the classroom and the out-of-classroom experiences?"—and that's what students have to think about a little more when going through this process.

They should not be overwrought over the fact there may be a couple of "C's" from their freshman year or that they aren't off the charts in terms of standardized tests because they're just not a good standardized test taker. Applicants allow themselves to get caught up in these issues and they don't focus on their strengths and what they can contribute here.

Every student we admit has certain deficiencies and shortcomings in his or her candidacy.

There's also a large concern on the part of prospective students that they need to make themselves different, that we evaluate people in certain neat categories or boxes like ethnicity, gender, geography, work experience, or educational background—and that's not the case. I don't know how many people I've admitted from consulting backgrounds or from Paris or from any number of different categories. My goal as an admissions officer is to build an applicant pool that is enormously diverse and once I have accomplished this, I can actually select the people who are most compelling within the applicant pool and not focus on these different categories. I don't think students believe that; they're sure [in their thinking] that "I've got four years of consulting experience, [so] I don't stand a chance because there are so many consultants out there applying for top-tier MBA programs."

As I said at the beginning, don't use your resume data to distinguish yourself; tell me about the impact of the experiences and the choices behind them and you will distinguish yourself. Also, this is a very time-consuming and difficult process (I always go back to my own experiences as a prospective student [he went to Wharton]) and I would tell applicants they need to think strategically about this process. You can't do a great job applying to eight or nine top-tier MBA programs; it's just too time-intensive and you need to focus on which schools are the best fit for you and maybe have a couple of long shots and a couple where you're comfortable you can be admitted. It's tough to juggle the application process and a very demanding work schedule as well.

As far as readers, there are three on average. Never less than two, usually three, oftentimes four or five. I find it very easy to get excited about the essays; it's easier in January or February than in April, and that's why the timing of applications is oftentimes very important. By waiting until the admissions deadline, applicants do compromise their chances at virtually any school.

Linda Baldwin
Director of Admissions
UCLA Graduate School of Management

THE ANDERSON SCHOOL AT UCLA is interested in admitting people, not credentials, and the essays are where you meet the people. We look for the degree of personal insight and energy that is demonstrated by applicants through the essays. From the essays we are able to discern who the applicants are, what they have accomplished, and the impact they have had on others, and we get an overall sense of how they will add value to and fit within our environment.

The essays require serious reflection. They play a critical role in placing other parts of the application into context. Among qualified applicants the essays serve the purpose of revealing who is most deserving, most appealing, and the best match for us. It is important to know that there is not a "right" answer. Attempts at second-guessing what the appropriate response should be or at sounding like everyone else won't get you admitted. Given the sizable applicant pool, those individuals who can bring forth their special qualities and unique experiences are admitted. The key is to write essays that reveal your thought process and distinct personality.

Aside from being a reflective process, the essays can also be extremely instructive. Sufficient time to think about the questions as well as to write and edit responses will alleviate much of the anxiety applicants have about this experience. Superficiality or redundancy detracts from the impact of the essays and fails to give us adequate opportunity to know the applicant. It is always important to respond to the questions being asked. Be honest and frank in your assessment of your strengths and weaknesses. The essays are the appropriate vehicle for clarifying a weakness or deficiency in your background. However, avoid making excuses.

Preparing the essays or at least spending some time thinking about the questions can be excellent preparation for an interview. At the very least, it will probably boost your confidence, and possibly you will be more at ease during the interview session.

Essays are read by at least two or three members of the admission committee. In addition to the admission officers, faculty, top-level administrators, alumni, and graduating students participate in the admission process.

Sally O. Jaeger
Director of Admissions
The Amos Tuck School (Dartmouth College)

WHAT WE'RE TRYING TO DO is get a sense of who this
person is. What are his or her interests, professional and personal?

That's one of the reasons we ask as many questions as we do and the kinds of questions we ask. Of equal importance is [the question] why is this person applying to business school, what are his or her reasons for applying for this very specific professional degree, what does he or she hope to gain from the two-year experience, where does he see this two-year experience taking him, what are the short- and long-term goals, why [is the applicant choosing to go] through this intense, very expensive process? Basically we want to know [the reasons] why. We want to know who this person is because we want to make sure that this is the right place for him or her. Tuck is a very small school and it's not the right place for everybody. I think someone who wants an anonymous business school experience—somebody who wants to come in, get the degree and get out—would be very unhappy here. This is a school, a community, an environment where people come in and have to get really involved to get the most out of their experience, so within our questions is a search for that sense of commitment, that sense of social responsibility, that sense of community that we offer. We're looking for those same feelings, those same beliefs, those same ideals in the individuals who apply to Tuck.

Our first essay is "Why do you want an MBA?" and it's probably one of the most important. One of applicants' biggest mistakes is that they don't see the big picture; they only see the small picture so they get involved in minutiae. They get too focused on what they've been doing, detail by detail. They just regurgitate or reiterate what they've been doing without much thought as to where they see themselves going. Clearly we're not expecting people to know what they want to be when they grow up, so to speak; we're not asking them to say [for example] they want to be working for corporate finance at Goldman Sachs in five years. We [do] want them to have a sense of where it is they want to be. What I tell people when I'm talking about our first essay is that we want them to be able to take their past and current professional experience, and show us how that has led them to this process of pursuing the MBA. How is their experience, combined with the two years at MBA school, going to take them where they want to go? Again, that doesn't have to be a specific job with a specific company, but it's an idea of where they're headed. They might have several possibilities, but these have to make sense; they can't [for example] tell us they want to go into consulting and investment banking and work for a not-for-profit. They have to be able to justify what they say. Clearly there has to be some experience in their background that leads them to this idea, this thought, this possibility.

Other mistakes include not answering our question or trying to be funny when the applicant [actually] is not. When an applicant writes an essay based on what he or she thinks we want to hear from him or her, not what he himself feels, that's a mistake. Applicants [have the opportunity within these essays to be] telling us a story that nobody else can tell; it's a big mistake if the applicant is not doing that. The whole point of the essay is to get to know who this applicant is as an individual. Other mistakes involve spelling errors and not proofreading the essays. People who don't know how to write well, who have

> ## The best essays that I've read are from people who've said they've learned a lot about themselves through this application process.

sentence fragments, who put apostrophes in the wrong place [are at a disadvantage].

Good essays require a lot of self-reflection. The best essays that I've read are from people who've said they've learned a lot about themselves through this application process. They've sat down and thought about why they're going through this process, what they want out of this program, and where they see themselves headed, so when it comes time to write the essays, everything flows. It's important to be yourself; don't try to be someone you're not. Don't spend a lot of time thinking about what the admissions officers want to read; think about what kinds of things you want the school to know about you, what's most important to you, because, ultimately, that's what's going to be most important to us when we make our decision.

Our process is a two-person evaluation; each application–regardless of GMAT, GPA–is evaluated thoroughly by two different people and then it's evaluated again a third time by me. So every application gets at least three looks and the number could be four or five. We have to get through 1,000 applications in a 4-to-6-week process. I love the essays because you learn so much about people. I feel I've read good essays if I've learned something new, something I didn't know before.

> ### Dr. Donald Martin
> Director of Admissions
> The University of Chicago
> Graduate School of Business

I THINK FIRST AND FOREMOST we want to get some
sense of the inside of an applicant's head and in particular what it is that is prompting this person to pursue a graduate education in business–what has led them to this point, what they think the MBA will do for them in terms of their educational desires and objectives as well as their career goals. That is certainly important to us. We want to know not only what they hope to get from the experience but also what they hope to contribute while they're with us. We have two other essays designed to be more fun to answer and these may help us get a certain sense of someone's creative side. All of the essays give us a sense of the applicant's written communication ability and also provide a dimension that is outside the more strictly objective demographic or academic data that we look at.

Mistakes? Sometimes because applicants are busy, they rush through the process and don't check their work for grammatical correctness, spelling, etc. The way in which someone prepares the work, just in terms of their presentation, can be very important. Sometimes they'll send the wrong essays to the wrong school, which certainly doesn't look real good. Or they take an essay written for another school, take that school's name out and put our school's name in. Then the essay almost sounds so generic that it doesn't mean a lot. Sometimes applicants think we have a certain idea of the kind of answer we want them to give on these questions, so they have to write accordingly. If they do that, it causes them to appear fake, not genuine. This causes us to be a little more skeptical than if someone simply answers the question in the best way he knows how and thus tends to be himself. I often tell applicants that yes, we are evaluators but we are not psychologists; these are not trick questions, we are not trying to "psych" anyone out, we just want to get to know you better. I've been in admissions for almost seventeen years now and one begins to be able to get a sense of when people are pulling your leg. If the personality and presentation are both good and real and genuine, that means a lot.

The best advice I can give—and I know this is easier said than

We look for reasons to admit people; we don't look for reasons to deny them.

done—is for applicants not to approach this process so seriously that they become paranoid about it and end up hurting themselves. This is about being yourself and doing the best you can to present an accurate picture of who you are. That will help admissions committees get a sense of whether you are really a good match for our school. We look for reasons to admit people; we don't look for reasons to deny them. Be honest and forthright and present yourself in the best way you can.

There are three readers. The first person is one of our first-year students who serves on what's called the dean's student admissions committee. We select about 100 people from our 500-member incoming class to read applications for us. They go through a very extensive reader training program with our staff in the month of October, which leads up to our first application deadline in November. They read the application first and fill out an entire reader's sheet on which they evaluate the applicant in several areas and then make a recommendation as to what decision should be made. Then that recommendation is taken out of the file and it goes to a full-time member of my staff—an associate or assistant director—who does a second identical read and fills out the same sheet; however, this staff member doesn't know what the first reader said. These two recommendations are placed back in the application, which then comes to me. I do review every one and I make the final decision after that. In some cases, I'll get another opinion if I think I need it.

Linda Meehan
Assistant Dean for Admissions and
Financial Aid
Columbia Business School

WE BREAK OUT THE APPLICATIONS into four separate categories: the interview; personal characteristics; the professional promise; and last, but certainly far from least, the academics. What we look for in the evaluatory interview is very much what a recruiter will look for in an MBA candidate when he's looking to hire someone. We're also looking for anything that will be in addition to what's on paper. Personal characteristics have to do with outside activities, leadership, motivation, what makes a person individual or unique. The next piece—which we will certainly pull from the essays—is the professional promise. We are looking for what the candidate has done, the level of responsibility, what they want to do, and how the MBA—particularly the Columbia MBA—is going to help them make that bridge from what they have done to what they want to do, both short- and long-term. We're really looking for focus, for people who really do have a sense of where they're headed. That's very, very important. Our first essay in particular is directed toward that. People who cannot fully define their short- and long-term goals (although they may not know the specific job) are probably not ready to apply to a business program. We need to know those goals to determine whether the applicants are realistic and whether Columbia is going to be able to help them reach those goals. The degree alone will not make a major career switch happen. As an undergraduate you have four years to kind of poke around; in graduate school you have only two years. If you have no clue of where you're headed, you're really not going to take advantage of an MBA program and, in particular, our program.

One of the things you want to do when you write the essays—and I'm gleaning this from a colleague of mine at another institution because she expressed this so well—is you want to come alive off the page and write the story that only you can write. When you write your essay, don't try to impress me, don't try to impress my committee; what you really want to do is help us know who you are and what may make

You want to come alive off the page and write the story that only you can write.

you different from the other 4,576 applicants. You are a unique individual and if you remember that and that your experience is unique to you, you'll be far more effective in writing your essays.

We're looking to make sure you can express yourself well with the written word: do you use proper grammar, do you know how to use spell-check and does the essay make sense? Read the questions very carefully and answer the question that we have asked. Make sure that you don't try to adapt another institution's essay question to us; we're very, very sensitive to that. Proofread your essay and make sure that at the end, when you say "I'm really dying to be at Columbia," you really write Columbia and not another institution by mistake. Keep yourself organized; be careful and thoughtful enough to be sure that you're supplying us with our application and our information. [Sometimes] applicants have their own agenda, which they're putting forth while forgetting what we have asked. Or they send in too much supplemental information. They need to be sensitive to the fact that the person who does the first read is probably also going to be reading 1,000 or 1,200 other applications. They need to be concise, do what we ask them to do. Think what you really want to write about and say, do it concisely and clearly, don't be afraid to reveal your personality and to tell us the story that only you can tell.

We work very hard to bring into each class a wide variety of backgrounds and people; as a result, we try to interview as many people as we possibly can. We have currently interviewed about 75 percent of our incoming class; we interviewed 60-percent-plus of the applicant pool and we're looking to do more. Ninety-nine percent of the interviews are done after the application has been received in our office [so it's helpful to applicants that they've gone through the essay-writing process first].

Each application is given a complete, thorough read by one person and then it goes to me and I review. Very often the application will then go to a third person—if there is no decision that is agreed upon—and it will go to the committee. On average each application is seen by at least three people and, very often, more.

Mary Miller
Director of Admissions and Aid
The Stern School of Business,
New York University

OUR ESSAY QUESTIONS are a little different from many other schools'. The first one, in which we ask about goals and career aspirations, is very similar. But we try to be a little more creative and relevant in our other two questions. In general what we're looking for are people who have well thought-out ideas, can express those ideas in an articulate, concise way, and can follow our directions (page limits). The essays need to be specific to the individual and share something of their orientation with the admissions committee. They should use good grammar and follow the basic rules that you learn when you write an essay. We are evaluating their communication skills and how they think.

Our third essay—where we ask students to describe themselves to their classmates—has become my favorite. Some applicants write very creative essays, but we have also received cassette recordings, video-tapes, games, puzzles, and poems. It's the variety of orientations and ways of expressing themselves which I think adds a certain creativity to the process. We're one of the few schools to do this, so it's not like a cut-and-paste [situation]. Seventy-five percent of the responses to this question are in written form but it's not the traditional essay.

Some essays are very, very personal and share information that I'm *amazed* they're willing to share—intimate details of their personal or family life or work life. I'm not saying it's inappropriate at all; sometimes it's very appropriate and very relevant. Other people are very good at giving a global perspective on a career or an industry and how they fit into that—and their essays can be very effective.

We're one of only a few schools that offer interviews only *after* we read an application, so we know a lot about the applicant before he or she ever walks into our office. It's a win-win situation for us and the applicant.

Mistakes? Not using spell-check. Also, I read essays that say "I know Wharton or Columbia or Tuck is the school for me"—and they're submitting these essays to us! It shows a lack of attention to detail. The other mistake is not doing your research. Sometimes when applicants talk about career goals, they are totally unrealistic and it's real obvious to the admissions committee that they don't have much knowledge of the industry they wish to enter. Again, that translates into a lack of attention to detail, a lack of thoroughness we're looking for from applicants. Sometimes they also haven't done enough research on Stern and cannot express why it is the right program for them.

Advice? Many times they miss an opportunity to use the resources at hand, to have other people read and react to the essays. They write in isolation, send them to various schools, and just assume they've done the best job. Applicants should take advantage of colleagues with whom they work or friends whom they respect to give them constructive feedback. Most writers will tell you that editing and rewriting are essential. Sometimes I feel that an essay I'm reading was composed in this way: the applicant sat down in front of a computer, wrote it, did spell-check, sent it in, and that was the last time he or she looked at it. You can tell when people have spent time and effort on their essays–it comes through loud and clear. The ultimate result applicants want is an offer of admission from every school to which they apply so the decision [about where to go] is theirs, not ours. It's really too bad if they say, "Oh, if only I would have [done something differently with the essays]." I want them to feel so confident when they apply that they think, "This is the best possible job I can do." They should make sure that they are presenting their very best.

A minimum of three people read every application–and sometimes it's many more than that. It's interesting: if we have a particularly difficult or interesting application and I'm not familiar with the industry, what they're talking about, or their orientation, I will ask a variety of people to read it. I can think of one case when we had an applicant from Turkey; I'm not that familiar with the Turkish culture and the opportunities there in the business sphere. So I was asking in all of these people–faculty and current students who had been there [to Turkey]–and that application had many reviews before a final decision was made.

Richard A. Silverman
Executive Director of Admissions
Yale School of Management

THERE'S NO SINGLE TYPE OF ESSAY we're looking for; there's no "correct" response to the essay questions we pose. What are we looking for? First, we're looking for information to fill in the blanks in a person's resume. We want to know what our applicants have done and what they want to do in the future, what their values are, and how they relate their values to their work. We're also interested in how they write. The form of the essays can be important, as well as the content. How applicants handle the English language is important—the ability to articulate their thoughts in a clear and concise way. In a school with a surplus of qualified candidates, decisions are made for reasons that can't be reduced to numbers or facts in some formulaic way. Essays help our Admissions Committee do what it must do, which is to reach reasoned, yet ultimately subjective, judgments. You will find if you inquire from school to school that the importance of the essays increases as the selectivity of the admissions process increases.

In one essay we ask students, in effect, to rationalize their past and connect it to their future. We call this the "career objectives" essay. It gives us hard information, but this is also a way of determining if applicants are capable of thinking reflectively—and synthetically—about themselves and their careers. Often, even the most intelligent, by traditional measures, are not.

Our second essay is about learning goals and is designed to provide information about the applicant's reasons for wanting to attend the Yale School of Management in particular. What does he or she expect to learn, and how will this learning be put to use?

One common "mistake" in essays is to narrate one's resume, or life history, without any reflection or evaluation or self-criticism. Another mistake is to write "what the Admissions Office wants to hear," which usually turns out to be very artificial sounding at best. There is also the person who is low-key to the point of not telling us very much. We call this the "British understatement problem." It's not always a mistake; in fact, it often makes for a refreshing change after countless self-glorifying essays (another pitfall). But in some cases an applicant simply doesn't say much, and we can't tell if it's because of modesty, lack of expressive ability, or possibly because he or she hasn't given much thought to what we're trying to do with the essays or with application information generally.

Advice? Don't send first drafts. Write essays and then sit on them for a while. Try to be as clear and concise as possible, but don't let the school's length limitations prevent you from being thorough. Between thoroughness and terseness there is a happy medium, however; and most essays are too long—or rather, more are too long than too short.

The best approach is simply to answer the school's questions as thoughtfully and honestly as you can. Let the admissions people make the admissions decisions. Don't try to psych out the process and make the decision for them. Don't try to pretend to be the stereotype that you think the school has in mind, because when you do that, you probably won't convey much of your own personality or your own thoughts.

Again, be honest. Honesty and openness are virtues in essay writing, as in work and life, as is (maybe) a little risk-taking. People often think that the only applicants who succeed in management school admissions are those who have very precise ideas of what they want to do with the next 40 years of their lives. You, in fact, might be rather indecisive at this stage of your life. You might be coming to a period of re-examination. You feel like retooling, turning a page, changing direction; but you don't yet know exactly which way you want to go. If that's the case, say so. We've been around a long time, and we understand quite well that some of our best students, and many future managerial leaders, go through this kind of "passage." It is much better to be honestly undecided about your future than falsely precise. On the other hand, vagueness is not a virtue, and it would be misleading not to say that most good applicants display in their essays a strong sense of purpose.

Judith Goodman
Assistant Dean, Admissions and
Student Services
University of Michigan School of
Business Administration

WE'RE LOOKING FOR A CLEAR, concise response. We're also looking for appropriate or correct English, good writing skills, and some indication of focus in career objective. We do not want to bring in someone who doesn't know yet what he or she wants to do. If the applicant is not sure if the next step should be the MBA degree, then that needs to be given careful consideration before he or she becomes a really viable candidate for the program.

Whatever the person wants to say in the essay is up to him or her. We bring individuals in, the class is heterogeneous; we're not looking for everyone to fit in the same mold.

Whatever the question is, we want to see that they've thought the answer through and that it makes sense in terms of the way they've stated it. They need to understand what the MBA. can do for them and maybe what it cannot do as well.

Typical mistakes are technical or grammatical errors. Some of these we can forgive because some of them are typos. I think sometimes the individual is not as concise as he or she should be; sometimes, however, they're too short in their response.

A person should plan to have enough time because it is usually a difficult process. You do need to feel motivated and creative when you sit down to write or at least jot down some ideas. So, if you allow enough time, you can begin your thought process, make an outline, jot down ideas, come back to it, rewrite, and get it into what you think is the final form. It might not be a bad idea to have someone who knows you read the essays to see if they make sense. Then, if something is really askew in the thought process, you can try to clarify it. And critique it yourself for good grammar and structure.

If there is quick agreement, only two to three people will read each essay. If there is disagreement, then the entire committee would get involved, which means a total of four or five.

Joyce P. Curll
Assistant Dean for Admissions and
Financial Aid
Harvard Law School

I LOOK FOR A WELL-WRITTEN statement that conveys
coherent thoughts and ideas and that helps me know the applicant

better. I hope it will be interesting and that after reading it I will have a better sense of who the person is and what kind of student that person will be when he or she joins the class. The more a statement conveys how a person thinks, what he or she thinks is important, or other such insights, the better. You should think of the statement as an opportunity to round out pieces to the puzzle that makes up your application. Write about issues or problems you think about and how you have dealt with them. The more personal you can be—the more you can bring in your own background or history—the more valuable the statement can be.

To avoid mistakes you must walk the narrow line between being too cautious or too "creative" in the personal statement. If you are too cautious and only provide us a shopping list of such standard things as what you've done, where you've been, and why you want to go to law school, you may come across as bland or uninteresting, or fail to convey what kind of mind you have. A shopping list is frequently just a recapitulation of materials found elsewhere in the application and adds nothing of what the person would contribute to the class. If you are too creative, the statement can be too cute—attention-getting but not impressing.

I like to see an applicant willing to take a risk but comfortable with the material being presented. If you're ready to take a risk with an unusual approach, you should produce a high-quality result, and one with which you are comfortable. For example, the person who would like to send us some poetry would be well advised to send us a sample of poetry, indicating that poetry is important to him or her, rather than trying to turn the statement into a poem. An example of a high-risk, low-reward statement would be a statement in the form of a brief. The applicant may be trying to demonstrate knowledge of how to write a brief, but it is definitely not an original idea and loses impact with the contortions required to fit the format. Another example of a potential mistake is the urge to begin with a quote. We're more interested in what you have to say than in what you've found that some famous person or writer has to say. There are a limited number of relevant quotable quotes. Commonly, applicants have quoted de Tocqueville or Shakespeare. I can recall one person who quoted his grandmother, but now that it has been done it is no longer original.

Sometimes people get so involved in the thinking process that they will write very long-winded statements. Some of the best statements are quite short (a page or two) and to the point. The one or two one-sentence statements I have seen have not been effective.

Peel away the preconceived notions about what you think is expected, then think about what you want to convey to the committee and how that ties in with everything else in your application. Think about leaving the committee with an impression of you. Be comfortable with whatever you write. The personal statement is the only part of the application over which you have complete control when you apply to law school. Write it, take another look later, and then have someone who really knows you and whose judgment you trust read it and determine if it is reflective of who you are.

One of the more effective statements I have read was about ideas with which the applicant was wrestling. It was effective because it conveyed understanding of important philosophical issues and related them to external ideas and ideas with which the applicant had been engaged academically. Only a true intellectual can do this well.

In some of the most successful statements, applicants have reflected on who they are, what they're all about, and why they have done what they have done, and have left the committee with one or two thoughts about them. The personal statement is personal. In a way, it is like an interview that you control: You are the one who decides what the committee is going to ask you, and you're the one who responds. Consider that you have roughly 15 minutes with the committee, and that you have the opportunity to convey a message that they all will read. Think about any questions that might arise as a result of what you've written—as if you did have an interview based on that material—and answer those questions.

There are anywhere from two to six readers, depending on whether the first two people agree. Without consensus, the application is passed on to more readers. One year we had 8,500 applications, and there have been numerous years when we've had over 7,000. Our entering class is 540.

Edward Tom
Director of Admissions
University of California at Berkeley
School of Law (Boalt Hall)

WE'RE LOOKING FOR QUALITY of writing. And in terms of substance, we're looking for things that set the applicant apart from everyone else who will essentially have that individual's identical GPA and LSAT score. We view the personal statement as the applicant's opportunity to inform us of anything in particular that he or she might want the admissions committee to know.

We don't have a standard form; we leave it pretty open-ended. We do warn applicants that our job is to choose law students, not lawyers, so to that extent we're interested in their academic potential, not exactly why they want to go to law school or what they want to do with their law degree upon graduation (because people often change their minds). In some cases, applicants have some burning interest or a significant event in their lives that compels them to go to law school for a specific reason, or else they have volunteered or worked actively in some area that interests them very much. And in those cases, of course, they should talk about why they want to get into environmental law or why they want to do public interest. So there are always exceptions, but, in the main, people who don't have that experience or unique interest ought to be talking about how they are different from everybody else.

It's a mistake having a sentence saying "I've always wanted to go to Harvard Law School." Some applicants forget to do the change in their computer, so we get a personal statement really meant for another school. And it's surprising how many spelling and grammatical errors we get. The personal statement is very important to us; it's a reflection of the applicant and the care with which he or she approaches law school. It's really a representative piece of work.

Applicants should outline what they want to say in the personal statement and write clear, concise sentences, keeping in mind who their audience is and what our purpose is. I would stay away from trying to be cute. There's no really good substitute for a cogent sentence. Humor, unless it's done really well, often falls flat on its face.

Each and every application here is read at least once, and many of them may be read as many as three, four, or five times by as many different people. If an application passes the initial screening, it may go on to a second screening by an admissions committee (faculty and students who operate in teams of two).

Faye Deal
Director of Admissions
Stanford Law School

FIRST OFF, WE'RE LOOKING FOR a personal

statement that's very well written and well focused. There are a variety of things an applicant can write about; it does not have to be about why he or she wants to go to law school. I tell applicants who are in the process of writing that this is their one opportunity to tell the admissions committee why they're different from every other applicant in the pool, what makes them special and how they can stand out from the 4,000 other applicants we look at every year. It's not an easy task, but if they approach it this way, then they can focus their personal statement. What we don't want to see as we're reading the personal statements is just a review of something else that's already in their files. What I want to come away with is something new about the applicant that I haven't picked up from anywhere else in the file. If someone wants to focus on one particular job they've had and how that job has sort of led them down a certain path, that's fine but, again, we don't want just a reiteration of what the resume states.

Oftentimes I will tell applicants to treat the personal statement as though they were in an interview with us and we've just told them, "Tell us something about yourself" or "Tell us something that you think would make a difference in your file."

If someone is an older applicant who has been out working in a particular field and now is making the jump over to law school, that person should anticipate that one of the questions that's going to come up when we review the file is "Why is this person changing careers?" so that person may want to focus their personal statement on that. An applicant who was clearly premed the first couple of years of college and then changed to poli sci might want to tell us why; otherwise, that's an unanswered question we have.

Some applicants mistakenly think that in all cases what we want to know is why they want to go to law school, and that's not

> **If you're going to write a winning personal statement, you cannot do it in two or three hours; it requires a lot of thought.**

necessarily true. I've read many very good statements from applicants about some particular event in their life, their studies abroad while an undergraduate, or people they've met who have had an impact on their lives. I had a personal statement once from a woman [who ended up being a student at Stanford Law] who was a film major in college and told us about herself and wrote it as if she were filming it. There's a fine line between being creative and cautious, and I think it's hard for applicants to figure out exactly how far they can go and still have a good statement. The other day I read a personal statement that was written as though it were an LSAT exam and I thought that was a little too cutesy. Keep in mind that you're applying to a graduate program.

Mistakes? Sometimes, if their undergraduate record was not particularly strong, applicants make the mistake of focusing their whole personal statement on explaining away their undergraduate GPA. [In reality] there's nothing they can do about that, and that's not what the personal statement should be used for from our perspective. It should be a way to give us information that we wouldn't be able to glean from the rest of the application.

[Another mistake people make is] being too gimmicky or too creative. To make your personal statement a poem, for example, is a little gimmicky.

A number of applicants are surprised that we read the personal statement so completely. The misconception out there [sometimes fostered by misinformed prelaw advisers] is that the personal statement really doesn't matter, that it all comes down to the LSAT and the GPA—and that's not true at all. We could fill our class by the numbers but we don't. When you consider the quality of applicants and the few spaces we have to offer, if we have a numerically strong candidate but his writing skills are weak as evidenced through the personal statement, that person may not be offered a spot in the class.

The personal statement is obviously the most difficult part of the application. If you're going to write a winning personal statement, you cannot do it in two or three hours; it requires a lot of thought. Start way ahead of time and do several drafts, at least. When you think you've got your final draft, have someone who knows you well—whether it's a spouse, significant other, or a very good friend—take a look at it and ask this person if it rings true. I remember that one of our students told me he had his wife take a look at one draft and after reading it, she said, "You're not that arrogant." He wrote another one and she said, "You're not that humble, either." He reworked it, finally came up with a copy he liked and that his wife also thought [represented] what he was all about.

Keep in mind that part of the exercise is to say what you want to say and to do so in about two pages. Two pages should be enough to get your point across.

I read all the files and then there's also an actual committee composed of faculty members. Some files will only get one read, some will get as many as three reads.

> **Michael D. Rappaport**
> Dean, Admissions
> UCLA School of Law

APPLICANTS SHOULD TAKE THE TIME to look at what the law school is asking them to write about. At UCLA we say, "We know you have lots of extracurricular activities—we want to know how you differ, what makes you unique. What can you bring to the first-year class that's going to make you distinct from the other 99 people who are already there?" The fact that you were active in your fraternity or sorority is really not going to do it. What we're looking for is people who, in their personal statement, stand out as being so unusual, so diverse, that they're extremely attractive as law students for the first-year class. Maybe what's going to make someone distinctive is that he or she spent six months living in a log cabin in Alaska. You try to give the law school some justification for admitting you. With a lot of people, there's nothing that's going to make them distinctive. If that's the case, they've got to recognize that, indeed, the essay is not going to make that much difference here at UCLA.

We're also asking if there's any reason their LSAT or grades are not predictive. You'd be amazed at the number of people who completely ignore this—they don't take advantage of the opportunity.

Most law schools operate fairly similarly. There's a certain group of applicants whose grades and LSAT scores are so high that the presumption is that the applicants are going to be admitted unless they do something terribly stupid to keep themselves out. I have seen applicants whose personal statement has done that, but it's extremely rare. At the other extreme is another group of applicants who—no matter what they write—are not going to get in.

The applicant has to realize, first of all, where he or she stands. If you have a straight-A grade point average and a perfect LSAT score, you don't have to spend a lot of time worrying about your personal statement. On the other hand, if you know you're in the borderline area, that's where the personal statement becomes very, very important.

The applicant should take the time to read the application to see what the schools are asking for. Sometimes the school will ask for a general description of why you want to go to law school or why they should admit you, something of that nature. In such a case you can be fairly sure the school is just interested in the essay to see how well you write. So what you say isn't as important as how you say it. On the other hand, some schools are more specific—UCLA is a very good example of that.

Make sure the essay is grammatically and technically correct and well written. Avoid sloppy essays, coffee-stained essays, or essays that are handwritten so you can't read them. You'd be amazed at what we get!

Dennis Shields
Assistant Dean and Director of Admissions
University of Michigan Law School

THE ESSAYS GENERALLY ARE the method by which the candidate introduces himself to you because, for the most part, we know nothing about them except what the LSAT score is and what their academic record is like. Additionally, you may have a resume in front of you or a series of questions [whose answers] approximate what they would put on a resume. One of the first things you look for is who the person is and some sense of where they've been, what they've done, why they've done it, and some sense of why they're interested in going to law school. Second, I think law schools are interested in knowing what sort of contribution outside of the norm—that is, being hard-working, bright students—a particular candidate might bring to the legal education enterprise. Are they different in a way that is significant from other candidates and, if they are, how is that relevant? That may speak to race and ethnicity, the nature of their life experiences, their academic or socioeconomic background. We look in these essays for something that might tell us about them—how they're going to contribute in a way others might not. Third, you look for people who are able to communicate their thought process in a coherent, reasonably sophisticated manner. You have the LSAT score and their academic record, which give you some sense of what their intellectual abilities might be, but the essay ought to supplement that by showing they can think and write in a way that's fairly nuanced and sophisticated.

Mistakes? Applicants tend to make these essays long-winded resumes; in other words, their resumes might be an outline of what their essays are. When you get to law school, they don't pin a badge on you with your name and a list of all the things that you've done, so putting these things in a personal statement doesn't make any sense. [Within the application] you have a resume or a series of questions that elicit that information, so to recap all that again is redundant and often boring.

The essay should follow the directions in the application; if it asks for one page or 250 words, the applicant should try to stay within those boundaries. We have a reasonableness standard. Whoever sits down to read the applicant's file has probably, if they're lucky, half an hour to do it. So the candidate needs to make judgments about what's most important [to include]. Submitting a Ph.D. thesis, honors papers, multitudinous newspaper clippings [or other materials not requested] is something they shouldn't do. What candidates need to present is something that can be read carefully and digested in 15 to 30 minutes. Also, they ought to be themselves; they ought not to try to sway the reader by their apparent vocabulary and [use of] multi-syllable words. They're much better off being direct and succinct. The people who are reading these files have read a lot of other files, so they have a frame of reference with which to think about this [your statement]. You need to stay within this frame of reference: they know you have a college degree or are about to get one, that you might have some work history and they expect you to talk about things in that general vein. You don't want me to be reading your senior honors thesis on physics because I don't know much about that. So applicants need to get to the point and make sure that whatever they write is well-written, free of typographical errors, tailored to what the school asks for. They ought not to simply word-process their essay and send the same one to every school to which they apply. A fundamental judgment they have to make concerns what is a reasonable number of law schools to which to apply—four, five, six, seven, maybe as many as eight. Each essay ought to fit the parameters of what a particular school asks for. It's easy for me to pick up a file and know that Yale got the same essay that we did. You don't want to create a new one for each school from whole cloth but each essay should be a little more different than which law school it mentions by name. At Michigan, for example, we have three separate essays an applicant can write that address the concerns I mentioned in the beginning. So I think it's worth an applicant's while to pull those out and separate them.

One or two people read each essay at Michigan. Some schools have full committee deliberation on every file; at the other end [of the spectrum] you have the dean of admissions who essentially makes all the decisions. All law schools are somewhere on that continuum between those two poles but we're more toward the end where the dean of admissions essentially makes those judgments. I have a couple of professional staff members who aid me in reading files and making recommendations to me and then I ultimately make the judgments.

Albert R. Turnbull
Associate Dean for Admissions and Placement
University of Virginia School of Law

UNTIL ABOUT FOUR YEARS AGO, we used the stimulus, "Give us in 200 words or so your reason for wanting to go to law school." We became dissatisfied because the responses we were getting, particularly from undergraduates, were repetitive, bland, and not very helpful in getting a handle on the individual involved. Eventually, the stimulus became, "Write on a matter of interest to you," the purpose to be quite open-ended. Non-undergraduates still focus on why they're applying to law school at this particular time in their lives, but our new stimulus has produced a much more individualized and helpful addition to the application folder because oftentimes it tends to mesh with and complement the lists of extracurricular activities. We get a very wide range of approaches, from poems to essays on economics. We're looking for style and writing ability to some extent, as well as additional insight about the applicant.

Applicants make a mistake when they try to write something they think will please the committee. When they try to anticipate what that might be, they run a great danger of going astray.

The best statements we get reflect the individual in an honest, genuine, and effective manner and thereby project to us an additional dimension that may be inadequately developed in the rest of the application. A lot of time needs to be put in on the crafting of the essay once the applicant decides on the subject.

Of the 3,500 applications, every one gets at least one careful read by a professional admissions person on the admissions committee. The more complicated cases go on to second and third reviews and maybe more.

Jean Webb
Director of Admissions
Yale Law School

YALE LAW SCHOOL DOES NOT require a personal statement. We ask for a 250-word essay on a subject of any interest. If an applicant also wants to submit a personal statement, he or she is welcome to do so. We don't consider the application incomplete without the 250-word essay if the applicant sends something longer or sends a personal statement instead, but that's not what we've asked them to do—and faculty readers have varying opinions on the importance of the essay and the importance of following instructions. The 250-word essays are very short—approximately one double-spaced page—so we look to see how well people can express themselves in a short space. The essay ought to be well written, by which I mean that grammar, spelling, and organization should be right.

The essay ought to be authentic. An applicant ought not to write about something because he or she thinks that's what someone else wants to read. The applicant clearly should choose something in which he or she has an interest and perhaps some passion.

Four people typically read each essay.

David Trabilsy
Assistant Dean for Admissions
The Johns Hopkins University
School of Medicine

IN TERMS OF CONTENT, there's nothing specific that we're looking for. I strongly feel this is entirely within the purview of the applicant to determine. In meeting with premed students I do not make specific suggestions concerning the content of the essay. The essay may be used any way the applicant wishes, and we do see a variety of central themes and writing styles. With respect to the very basic construction of the essay, it should be neatly typed, it should not exceed the space provided on the application, and it should be proofread carefully. It's unfortunate when you see an essay that seems to have good content but numerous typos or grammatical problems. It should be well planned, well thought out. Also, I think that instead of just looking at the essay entirely from their own perspective—"how am I going to use this space?"—applicants should consider how it will appear to the reader. It should be an original piece, an honest expression of the applicant, although it's not a bad idea to have it proofread by a few people to check for typing or grammatical errors.

On occasion we'll get applicants who don't fill out the essay, thinking it's an optional or unimportant part of the application, which it isn't. Using the essay can be helpful; candidates should take advantage of the opportunity to express themselves fully rather than giving a short response. When you see only a couple of sentences, it's not too helpful because we're not getting very much information. On the other hand, they shouldn't feel compelled to fill in the space entirely. Conversely, sometimes we see microscopic reductions of typing print in order to fit in additional information.

By a well thought-out essay, I don't just mean a free flow of thoughts but good construction from beginning to end. There isn't

> ## We read 3,000 or more applications each year. We get quite a variety of essays, and I wouldn't want it any other way.

necessarily a correct way of writing the essay; it's very open-ended. This is, perhaps, the only opportunity that applicants will have for us to know about them personally in some way, prior to when interview decisions are made. It enables applicants to express themselves and show they can write in a coherent manner. If statements are made about special skills or talents, they should be backed up with concrete evidence of academic work or extracurricular activities. On occasion we've seen anatomical drawings, caricatures, etc. Obviously, the intent is to catch the eye of the reader. Sometimes it may be effective, sometimes it isn't.

The essay may be read closely by a number of people at the front end when decisions are being made about interviews. Then it will be seen by the entire admissions committee after the interview is conducted. It could be a dozen or more people. We read 3,000 or more applications each year. We get quite a variety of essays, and I wouldn't want it any other way.

Dr. Gerald S. Foster
Director of Admissions
Harvard Medical School

I LOOK FOR AN ESSAY that's neat, literate, and not too long. We count the personal statement a lot more than the essay written on the AMCAS test, which turns out not to be very helpful. So you should give a personal statement some thought. I think there are all kinds of approaches. I think the important thing is for the essay to be a reflection of the student and demonstrate good written communication skills.

Some applicants try to include much too much. Every personal statement request indicates the things that the committee wants you to talk about, so the applicants should address those things and make the essay interesting for the reader.

We ask people to comment on some of the experiences and interests that bear on their choice of medicine as a career. People simply ought to write something that's revealing about themselves. What's written should be an honest representation of the writer and not something artificial that's done to satisfy a reader. Turnoffs? A statement that is unduly long or unduly self-congratulatory.

Two to three people read the statement to make a decision about an interview, and then, if the person is interviewed, the statement will be seen by everybody on the committee. There are about 15 people on the interviewing subcommittee. If the applicant moves on to become a finalist, then another 15 people will see the statement. I often read the personal statement before I interview somebody; it lets the applicant know I've read his or her folder, and it often gives me some opening subjects to discuss in the interview.

Dr. Andrew G. Frantz
Chairman, Committee on Admissions
College of Physicians and Surgeons
(Columbia University)

WE LOOK FOR HONESTY (as far as we can discern it), simplicity, straightforwardness. I tend to be put off by too many self-congratulatory statements, such as, "I'm an excellent candidate for medical school; I have great compassion"—that kind of thing. One person wrote, "As part of my personality, I radiate a high degree of warmth and sincerity"—and that was not good.

Try to sound natural. A lot of students would like to think that maybe they can somehow talk themselves into medical school, especially if their application is otherwise average or mediocre. They think there's some golden combination of words that, if only they can find it, will unlock the doors and get them in. I just don't think that's true.

It shouldn't be too long. Our application forms have a certain amount of space, and we prefer that the candidates don't go over that. Some people seem afflicted with a desire to write novel-length statements and those are difficult to read. Why do most people want to become doctors? They want to help other people, they're interested in science, and medicine seems to represent a good combination of both these impulses. Making the whole statement too lengthy or too flowery doesn't do them any good. Grammatical mistakes are bad. Spelling mistakes I tend to forgive because spelling is not perfectly correlated with intelligence, and even people who are quite bright can make spelling mistakes. But if it's full of spelling mistakes, that's not encouraging.

Our form used to ask, "Why do you want to be a doctor?," but eight or nine years ago we changed it to, "What satisfaction do you expect to receive from being a doctor?" A lot of people don't answer it; they just write their standard essay.

Some students have told me that they plan to spend a good part of their summer working on their essay, and I think that's nonsense. My own feeling is that the essay has been more a cause of people getting downgraded than being favorably judged, usually because it is too contrived or patently insincere. As an admissions committee member, after you've gone through thirty or forty such applications in an afternoon, you're so grateful for somebody who just says something simply and straightforwardly. The poor people who are reading these don't want highly wrought compositions.

Dr. Thomas Lentz
Assistant Dean for Admissions
Yale University School of Medicine

WE SIMPLY ASK FOR A PERSONAL profile, which is pretty open. It allows applicants to say whatever they want to say about themselves, what they would like to bring to the attention of the admissions committee. Most of the time people discuss their reasons for being interested in medicine. Others may discuss particular interests or hobbies or accomplishments. People also use it to explain deficiencies in their application. We view the personal profile as a supplement that the student perhaps can use to enhance his or her application.

People sometimes write an unusual type of essay, and they do it intentionally, I'm sure, to draw attention to themselves. For example, they'll tell a story or they'll write a poem. I have mixed feelings about this. Occasionally, some of these verge on the bizarre and make you wonder about the stability of the applicant. A few of them, though, are quite good and creative. You've got thousands of applications, and 90 percent of the essays sound the same, so some people will try to be different.

Be forthright and honest, and explain sincerely why you want to become a physician. If you can convey some of that desire and motivation through the essay, that might help a little bit.

Two people see the statement initially and then—if the person is to be interviewed—two more people who will do the interview. In our system, the interviewers will summarize the application to the committee, and occasionally they will call attention to something in the essay if it's particularly good or bad.

Lili Fobert
Director of Admissions
UCLA School of Medicine

YOU DO LOOK FOR MOTIVATION because the Personal Comments (section) is the only place the applicants have to indicate this. In other words, why are they interested in medicine? I don't think there's anything else specifically that we look for, other than whatever the applicant wants to tell about himself or herself.

The essay is read at UCLA by our screening committee, which is composed of about 25 people. Of course, each essay may not, necessarily be read by every person on the committee.

OTHER SELECTED GRADUATE PROGRAMS

Ruth Miller
Former Director of Graduate Admissions
The Woodrow Wilson School of Public and
International Affairs (Princeton University)

IT'S POSSIBLE TO REDEEM YOURSELF (in certain cases) or to kill your chances of admission with the personal statement. What's most important to me is for the candidate to make a compelling case for himself or herself. I want to be persuaded that I should admit this person. Good writing is important in this regard. Secondly, I look for the person's sense of what our program is all about and why it makes sense in terms of his or her career plans. We ask for two essays. One is a personal statement of motivation—why you want to come. It's supposed to be about 1,000 words (as is the public policy memorandum we also require). I want to get a sense of what the applicant is all about. First, they should tell me where they're coming from—what it is in their background that leads them to apply to a program like ours. Second, they should tell me what it is they want to get out of our program. Third, I want to know where they hope our program will eventually take them in their career. We want to get a sense of the person's commitment to the world of public affairs, whether they're interested in housing in the inner city or development in the Third World. It's important for us to know that an applicant is not simply motivated by making large sums of money. They may end up doing that, but we want to see some kind of commitment to making the world a better place. Now that's a really corny thing to say, but that is the underlying philosophy.

"I was a foreign service brat and grew up all over the world and that's what made me interested in international affairs" might be part of the personal part of someone's essay. But I don't need to know about their relationship with their brother. (There are cases, though, in which the applicant's personal life has a very direct bearing on why he or she wants to come to the Woodrow Wilson School.)

There are two common mistakes applicants make. An applicant will do a standard essay for half a dozen schools on a word processor and adapt it slightly for each school. But then one may forget to change one of the school names. There is nothing more irritating than reading a long essay that concludes with "And that's why I want to go to the Kennedy School at Harvard"–and you're sitting here on the Woodrow Wilson School admissions committee! The other mistake people make is talking about something they know nothing about. They'll say, "I want to do something in international relations," without indicating that they have any idea of what that means. Or, "I want to go and cure the problems in the Middle East" or, "I want to go and work for the United Nations"–those kinds of grandiose statements that indicate to me that the person really doesn't know the realities of career opportunities in this field; they might just as well tell me they want to be Secretary General of the United Nations. This is a very common mistake and the younger the applicant, the more likely he or she is to make it. I also don't like to get a sense that the applicant has dashed off the statement in 20 minutes and hasn't given much thought to it. Ours is a very, very competitive admissions situation–we get about 600 applications and make only about 80 offers of admission–and the personal essay is the one opportunity to tell the admissions committee why you want to come and why we should accept you over the next person who is equally well qualified academically. You have to distinguish yourself in some way. And you really have to let the admissions committee know what it is about this program in particular that interests you. For example, you could mention that you like that there is a small core of required analytical courses here at the Woodrow Wilson School and that then you're free to select a field of concentration and build up a substantive background in that field. Now if I read something like that, I would know that the applicant had read our catalog and understood what our curriculum was about and what was distinctive about our program. You need to write well, and check grammar, spelling, and punctuation. You also definitely need to type or do the application on a word processor. The days of handwritten career statements are over. The only way I would even want to accept something like that would be if the applicant is in the Peace Corps in Zaire and doesn't have access to a typewriter or word processor. But I get very annoyed with a handwritten career statement in any other circumstance. Also, avoid cuteness; we've had people who have done career statements in the form of a miniplay, for example. You want to sound like a professional, even though we know you're not in many cases. It's a really different process from applying to undergraduate college. You don't want to sound naive; that doesn't mean you don't want to sound idealistic, because many of the people who write to us impress us with their commitment and sense of dedication.

As director of graduate admissions, I read all of the statements, and I screen out about half of them. One other person reads those I've screened out just to double-check me. So the applicant's file may be read by as few as two people. If you are admitted, your file will have been read by a minimum of 6 people and could be read by as many as 14 (everyone on the admissions committee).

Professor Stephen Yenser
Vice Chair of Graduate
Studies/English
UCLA

I THINK THE FIRST THING that strikes me is the hardest to define, and that is style. I look for a certain turn of phrase, a certain wit, the unexpected and pleasing, and this can be arrived at in many different ways. What I look for in any distinguished writing is energy, imagination, originality, a gift for figure, for trope.

Next is the candidate's view of his or her career, especially these days, when the job market is so tight and diminishing. I want to know that the student is really committed to studying English literature and is aware of the possibility that there will not be a job available at the end of the line. So I want a sense of commitment, a sense of discipline, and a sense specifically of what the student wants to do. I don't think it's advisable for anyone to write that he or she just loves English literature and wants to read and write. People have to know what field they want or are most likely to work in, or what specific kinds of projects they want to pursue in a field—maybe even what the topic of the dissertation would be.

If I sense that a candidate is just filling out half a page cursorily—just doing the personal statement pro forma—and has not put much time or imagination into it, that's the kiss of death. Usually a straight autobiography should be avoided, although interesting and pertinent autobiographical facts should doubtless be included. But the statement should be more future-oriented than past-oriented. I don't really want the story of a student's life (although there are exceptions)

Applicants should try to find a way to enjoy writing the statement. They should get interested in the statement; they should want to write it.

but rather plans for and a vision of the future.

Applicants should try to find a way to enjoy writing the statement. They should get interested in the statement; they should want to write it. Write the statement and then run it beneath the cold gaze of someone who is familiar with this genre and can offer suggestions for revision (a former professor, in most cases). Ask for a rigorous critique, listen to what the professor has to say, and then revise it accordingly. It doesn't do any good to show it to a friend or a parent; it's got be somebody who is used to this genre and who has been impressed—and bored—by such statements before.

It sometimes helps for the student to have done some research on the university being applied to. If, for example, a student is applying to UCLA and really wants to come here because of our connections with the Clark Library and its resources, it's good for us to know this. Now one can also identify pretty readily somebody whose acquaintance with the special resources at UCLA comes simply by way of the brochure we send to all interested applicants. So it should be in-depth and true knowledge of the resources rather than a superficial knowledge.

We have three readers. We have a graduate committee of about seven, now broken down into about three subcommittees.

Erik Antonsson
Chairman, Graduate Admissions Committee,
Applied Mechanics, Civil Engineering &
Mechanical Engineering
California Institute of Technology

WE LOOK FOR SEVERAL THINGS. The statement provides some insight into how capable a student is in the English language. It's the first thing that jumps out when you read it, but it's the smaller of the two effects of the statement. I think the main thing is to see whether the student is aware of and has thought about the field to which he or she is applying; these are graduate applicants so I think this is a reasonable issue to try to discern. Does he or she know anything at all about it, has this person identified some of the key issues that are active in research, and does he or she have some familiarity with issues in the field? At the high end would be someone who might have even read a little bit of the literature or who is—through his or her undergraduate work—maybe familiar with some of the research going on currently in the area. At the low end would be somebody who just says, for example, "Gee, biomechanics is cool." So from the statement comes some insight about how serious a student is about a particular research area.

Some students genuinely don't know what they want to do and I think that's a good thing in a newly-applying graduate student. So I don't want to discourage anyone by saying I think students should have this clarity of purpose so finely honed that they know exactly what subtopic they're going to work on; that isn't the point. But even if they're not sure, there will generally be some area—or several areas—of interest and, again, I would look for the student to have something knowledgeable or sensible to say about those fields.

It doesn't help me to know the applicant has won 3,000 awards (that can be indicated elsewhere in the application); I want to see something about how the applicant thinks.

Mistakes? Dwelling on past accomplishments as opposed to describing future interests. The recitation of past accomplishments, prizes won and scores gotten—all that kind of stuff—is helpful but at the stage when we're reading the statement, we know all the applicants are highly qualified; that is almost beside the point. What we're looking for

> ## It doesn't help me to know the applicant has won 3,000 awards (that can be indicated elsewhere in the application); I want to see something about how the applicant thinks.

at that stage is, again, some insight into how the student thinks, what sort of clarity of purpose he has into one or more research areas. More serious mistakes come in composing English language sentences and paragraphs; students [sometimes] write sentences that aren't cogent and don't hang together. Probably more than half our applicants are nonnative English speakers, so we see varying degrees of skill in English. However, the worst examples of English language usage are not confined to the nonnative English language speakers. We get many applicants from the United States for whom English is clearly a serious obstacle. The statement gives us an opportunity to see how well a student can express himself, both in forming thoughts and in using the English language. Like it or not, we conduct our classes in English, our publications (with very few exceptions) all go out in the English language, and the oral examinations, as well as the written ones, are conducted in English. So I don't think it's unreasonable to expect a certain level of proficiency and to see that in the statement.

Advice? Have someone else read it, preferably someone with some familiarity with the process of applying to U.S. graduate schools. If there's a professor at your school that you could ask to read through your statement at the draft stage, by all means do that. I don't think the U.S. students do that anywhere near as much as they should; I can't gauge how much it's done in foreign lands. A certain amount of critique by, perhaps, someone more senior than the applicant and who may know universities reasonably well, can provide some thoughts on how to construct such a statement, how to make the language read clearly, what to emphasize and what not to emphasize. Brevity is also crucial. We do not usually read past the end of the second page of any applicant's statement.

Typically, three admissions committee members read each applicant's statement. Sometimes there are four or as many as five, depending on the department to which the applicant applies.

Professor Paul Green
Director, Master's Degree Program
Department of Biological Sciences,
Stanford University

WE LOOK FOR SOME RESEARCH experience and some ability to assign proper values to various kinds of activities. In other words, can they distinguish important problems from trivial problems? We don't care particularly what they've done, but they should provide some evidence of judgment. They need to have some sense of proportion about the structure of the scientific community, the academic community, or the industrial/commercial community (depending on just what their ambitions are). We look for students who wish to make fundamental contributions. They usually say what they've done and what they would like to do, and we read both parts carefully. I think there's a full page provided in the form, but they're free to add other pages and they often do. We check to what extent the statement corresponds with letters of recommendation because often applicants will talk about their work and we'll have a letter from the person under whom they did the work.

I would say it's a mistake to fill up that page with details of the buffers they used in order to extract the rat liver; they should display a sense of proportion, they should know that we don't care what the concentration of calcium chloride was, and so on. Anybody with any judgment would realize that's a waste of our time. Often they praise the institution–referring to our "outstanding" this and "outstanding" that–and this is pretty much a useless exercise. If the statements are vacuous and full of platitudes, that's obviously a negative. If they can't be explicit about future plans, they should at least give some example of the kind of thing they consider important.

As they look back on their past, the applicants should extract the value of their efforts. In some cases, the efforts might not have been successful but the applicant can, above all, be honest and say "We tried this project; it didn't work and we learned why. Nonetheless, I like to do science, etc. . . ." It's just as effective to read an intelligent analysis of something that didn't work as a recital of a lot of things that did. It is the analytical capability that counts. And the same for future plans, as I indicated before; there should be some sense of proportion about what counts and a realization that you have to balance effort against reward: you want to maximize reward per unit of effort; some sense of ability to do that is looked for. You should avoid being overly colorful or cute. Somebody wrote, "What I like doing most is people." Well, that sort of makes you ill. So I'd say don't be too cute, don't be too boring, and show some analytical, interpretive skills.

Three or four people read each statement.

APPENDIX

On the following pages, you will find two separate questionnaires: one to hand out prior to writing your personal statement, the other to hand out afterward. These surveys will enable you to secure valuable input from friends, family, colleagues, professors, or others who know you. You can also benefit from carefully reviewing these questions and will find the second questionnaire to be an excellent means of assessing the worthiness of your initial effort. Just remember that there is no substitute for the careful thinking and self-examination you must do on your own.

PREPARATORY QUESTIONNAIRE

I am applying to _____ and must prepare a personal statement as a part of that process. I want to be sure to include all relevant data about myself and my background, so I am soliciting information from various individuals who know me and whose judgment I value. Thank you for your help.

1. What do you think is most important for the admissions committee to know about me?

2. What do you regard as most unusual, distinctive, unique, and/or impressive about me (based on our association)?

3. Are you aware of any events or experiences in my background that might be of particular interest to those considering my application to graduate school?

4. Are there any special qualities or skills that I possess that tend to make you think I would be successful in graduate school and/or the profession to which I aspire?

PREPARATORY QUESTIONNAIRE

I am applying to _____ and must prepare a personal statement as a part of that process. I want to be sure to include all relevant data about myself and my background, so I am soliciting information from various individuals who know me and whose judgment I value. Thank you for your help.

1. What do you think is most important for the admissions committee to know about me?

2. What do you regard as most unusual, distinctive, unique, and/or impressive about me (based on our association)?

3. Are you aware of any events or experiences in my background that might be of particular interest to those considering my application to graduate school?

4. Are there any special qualities or skills that I possess that tend to make you think I would be successful in graduate school and/or the profession to which I aspire?

PREPARATORY QUESTIONNAIRE

I am applying to _____ and must prepare a personal statement as a part of that process. I want to be sure to include all relevant data about myself and my background, so I am soliciting information from various individuals who know me and whose judgment I value. Thank you for your help.

1. What do you think is most important for the admissions committee to know about me?

2. What do you regard as most unusual, distinctive, unique, and/or impressive about me (based on our association)?

3. Are you aware of any events or experiences in my background that might be of particular interest to those considering my application to graduate school?

4. Are there any special qualities or skills that I possess that tend to make you think I would be successful in graduate school and/or the profession to which I aspire?

PREPARATORY QUESTIONNAIRE

I am applying to _____ and must prepare a personal statement as a part of that process. I want to be sure to include all relevant data about myself and my background, so I am soliciting information from various individuals who know me and whose judgment I value. Thank you for your help.

1. What do you think is most important for the admissions committee to know about me?

2. What do you regard as most unusual, distinctive, unique, and/or impressive about me (based on our association)?

3. Are you aware of any events or experiences in my background that might be of particular interest to those considering my application to graduate school?

4. Are there any special qualities or skills that I possess that tend to make you think I would be successful in graduate school and/or the profession to which I aspire?

EVALUATIVE QUESTIONNAIRE

I have composed the attached personal statement(s) for submission to _____, which I hope to attend. If you could take some time to read what I have written and answer the following questions, I would be most grateful for the benefit of your perspective.

1. Did my opening paragraph capture your attention?

2. Did you find the statement as a whole to be interesting?

3. Did you find it to be well written?

4. Did it seem positive, upbeat?

5. Did it sound like me?

6. Do you regard it as an honest and forthright presentation of who I am?

7. Did it seem to answer the question(s)?

8. Can you think of anything relevant that I might have inadvertently omitted?

9. Is there material within the statement that seems inappropriate?

10. Did you gain any insight about me from reading this?

11. Did you notice any typos or other errors?

12. Do you think the statement has in any way distinguished me from other applicants?

13. Do you think my application to _____ is logical?

EVALUATIVE QUESTIONNAIRE

I have composed the attached personal statement(s) for submission to
_____, which I hope to attend. If you could take some time to
read what I have written and answer the following questions, I would
be most grateful for the benefit of your perspective.

1. Did my opening paragraph capture your attention?

2. Did you find the statement as a whole to be interesting?

3. Did you find it to be well written?

4. Did it seem positive, upbeat?

5. Did it sound like me?

6. Do you regard it as an honest and forthright presentation of who I am?

7. Did it seem to answer the question(s)?

8. Can you think of anything relevant that I might have inadvertently omitted?

9. Is there material within the statement that seems inappropriate?

10. Did you gain any insight about me from reading this?

11. Did you notice any typos or other errors?

12. Do you think the statement has in any way distinguished me from other applicants?

13. Do you think my application to _____ is logical?

EVALUATIVE QUESTIONNAIRE

I have composed the attached personal statement(s) for submission to _____, which I hope to attend. If you could take some time to read what I have written and answer the following questions, I would be most grateful for the benefit of your perspective.

1. Did my opening paragraph capture your attention?

2. Did you find the statement as a whole to be interesting?

3. Did you find it to be well written?

4. Did it seem positive, upbeat?

5. Did it sound like me?

6. Do you regard it as an honest and forthright presentation of who I am?

7. Did it seem to answer the question(s)?

8. Can you think of anything relevant that I might have inadvertently omitted?

9. Is there material within the statement that seems inappropriate?

10. Did you gain any insight about me from reading this?

11. Did you notice any typos or other errors?

12. Do you think the statement has in any way distinguished me from other applicants?

13. Do you think my application to _____ is logical?

EVALUATIVE QUESTIONNAIRE

I have composed the attached personal statement(s) for submission to _____, which I hope to attend. If you could take some time to read what I have written and answer the following questions, I would be most grateful for the benefit of your perspective.

1. Did my opening paragraph capture your attention?

2. Did you find the statement as a whole to be interesting?

3. Did you find it to be well written?

4. Did it seem positive, upbeat?

5. Did it sound like me?

6. Do you regard it as an honest and forthright presentation of who I am?

7. Did it seem to answer the question(s)?

8. Can you think of anything relevant that I might have inadvertently omitted?

9. Is there material within the statement that seems inappropriate?

10. Did you gain any insight about me from reading this?

11. Did you notice any typos or other errors?

12. Do you think the statement has in any way distinguished me from other applicants?

13. Do you think my application to _____ is logical?

ABOUT THE AUTHOR

Richard J. Stelzer is a consultant who advises a wide array of clients on winning strategies for written presentations.

He is also an author with numerous journalistic credits. His first book, *The Star Treatment*, examined the personal problems and experiences in psychotherapy of 23 well-known personalities.

Mr. Stelzer was graduated from Vanderbilt University and holds a master's degree in journalism from the University of Missouri.

Mr. Stelzer has worked in both advertising and public relations. He lives in West Los Angeles, California.

NOTES